Salvage

THE COAST OF UTOPIA PART III

Tom Stoppard's other work includes *Enter a Free Man, Rosencrantz and Guildenstern Are Dead, The Real Inspector Hound, Jumpers, Travesties, Night and Day, Every Good Boy Deserves Favour* (with Andre Previn), *After Magritte, Dirty Linen, The Real Thing, Hapgood, Arcadia, Indian Ink* and *The Invention of Love*. His radio plays include: *If You're Glad, I'll Be Frank, Albert's Bridge, Where Are They Now?, Artist Descending a Staircase, The Dog It Was That Died* and *in the Native State*. His work for television includes *Professional Foul* and *Squaring the Circle*. His film credits include *Empire of the Sun, Rosencrantz and Guildenstern Are Dead*, which he also directed, *Shakespeare in Love* (with Marc Norman) and *Enigma*.

TOM STOPPARD

Salvage

THE COAST OF UTOPIA
PART III

Grove Press
New York

First published in hardback and paperback in 2002 by Faber and Faber Limited, London, England

Printed in the United States of America

FIRST AMERICAN EDITION

Library of Congress Cataloging-in-Publication Data
Stoppard, Tom.
  Salvage / Tom Stoppard.
    p. cm. — (Coast of Utopia ; pt. 3)
  ISBN 0-8021-4006-8 (pbk.)
  ISBN 0-8021-1762-7 (hc)
  ISBN 0-8021-4003-3 (boxed set)
    1. Herzen, Aleksandr, 1812–1870—Drama. 2. Ogarev, N. P. (Nikolaæi Platonovich), 1813–1877—Drama. 3. Bakunin, Mikhail Aleksandrovich, 1814–1876—Drama. 4. Russians—England—Drama. 5. London (England)—Drama. 6. Revolutionaries—Drama. I. Title.
PR6069.T6S355 2003
822'.914—dc21

                                                                        2003042191

Grove Press
841 Broadway
New York, NY 10003
03 04 05 06 07   10 9 8 7 6 5 4 3 2 1

I am gratefully indebted to Trevor Nunn
for encouraging me towards some additions
and subtractions while *The Coast of Utopia*
was in rehearsal

ACKNOWLEDGMENTS

I would like to thank, first, Aileen Kelly, who has written extensively about Alexander Herzen and Mikhail Bakunin. I am indebted to her for her kindness as well as her scholarship. Moreover, Dr Kelly is, with Henry Hardy, who also has my gratitude for our exchanges, the coeditor of the book which was my entry to the world of *The Coast of Utopia*, namely *Russian Thinkers*, a selection of essays by Isaiah Berlin. Berlin is one of two authors without whom I could not have written these plays, the other being E. H. Carr, whose *The Romantic Exiles* is in print again after nearly seventy years, and whose biography of Bakunin deserves to be. I received valuable help from Helen Rappaport on Russian matters in general. I am particularly indebted to her for Russian translation, including lines of dialogue. Krista Jussenhoven kindly made up for my deficiency in German, Rose Cobbe corrected my French, and Sonja Nerdrum supplied me with the lines in Italian. My thanks to all of them, and to the Royal National Institute for the Deaf for access to its library.

SALVAGE was first performed in the Olivier Auditorium of the National Theatre, London, as the third part of *The Coast of Utopia* trilogy, on 19 July 2002. The cast was as follows:

ALEXANDER HERZEN   Stephen Dillane

SASHA HERZEN   Dominic Barklem/Alexander Green/William Green/Ashley Jones

MARIA FOMM   Anna Maxwell Martin

TATA HERZEN   Alexandra Thomas-Davies/Francesca Markham/Samantha Thompson

GOTTFRIED KINKEL   Nick Sampson

JOANNA KINKEL   Felicity Dean

MALWIDA VON MEYSENBUG   Eve Best

CAPTAIN PEKS   Sam Troughton

ALPHONSE DE VILLE   Jack James

ALEXANDRE LEDRU-ROLLIN   David Verrey

LAJOS KOSSUTH   Martin Chamberlain

MAZZINI   Richard Hollis

ERNEST JONES   Iain Mitchell

KARL MARX   Paul Ritter

ARNOLD RUGE   John Nolan

STANISLAW WORCELL   John Carlisle

LOUIS BLANC   Will Keen

MRS BLAINEY   Janine Duvitski

OLGA HERZEN   Clemmie Hooton/Alice Knight/Harriet Lunnon/Casi Toy

PARLOURMAID Janet Spencer-Turner

CIERNECKI Richard Hollis

A POLISH ÉMIGRÉ Sarah Manton

MICHAEL BAKUNIN Douglas Henshall

EMILY JONES Jennifer Scott Malden

ZENKOWICZ John Nolan

TCHORZEWSKI Kemal Sylvester

NICHOLAS OGAREV Simon Day

NATALIE OGAREV Lucy Whybrow

SASHA HERZEN AS AN ADULT Sam Troughton

IVAN TURGENEV Guy Henry

TATA HERZEN OLDER Anna Maxwell Martin

OLGA HERZEN OLDER Madeleine Edis/Ruth Jones/ Charlotte Nott Macaire

MARY SUTHERLAND Charlotte Emmerson

NICHOLAS CHERNYSHEVSKY Raymond Coulthard

HENRY SUTHERLAND Lewis Crutch/Freddie Hale/Thomas Moll/Greg Sheffield

DOCTOR Sam Troughton

PAVEL VETOSHNIKOV Nick Sampson

PEROTKIN Martin Chamberlain

SEMLOV Jack James

SLEPTSOV Jonathan Slinger

KORF Thomas Arnold

LIZA Alexandra Thomas-Davies/Francesca Markham/
Samantha Thompson

TERESINA Rachel Ferjani

TATA HERZEN AS AN ADULT Anna Maxwell Martin

OLGA HERZEN AS AN ADULT Jasmine Hyde

Director Trevor Nunn

Set, Costume and Video Designer William Dudley

Lighting Designer David Hersey

Associate Director Stephen Rayne

Music Steven Edis

Movement Director David Bolger

Sound Designer Paul Groothuis

Company Voice Work Patsy Rodenburg

CHARACTERS

ALEXANDER HERZEN, *a Russian exile*

SASHA HERZEN, *his son*

TATA HERZEN, *Herzen's daughter*

OLGA HERZEN, *Herzen and Natasha's daughter*

MARIA FOMM, *a German nanny*

GOTTFRIED KINKEL, *a German exile*

JOANNA KINKEL, *his wife*

MALWIDA VON MEYSENBUG, *a German exile*

ARNOLD RUGE, *a German exile*

KARL MARX, *a German communist in exile*

ERNEST JONES, *an English radical*

ALEXANDRE LEDRU-ROLLIN, *a French socialist in exile*

LOUIS BLANC, *a French socialist in exile*

STANISLAW WORCELL, *a Polish nationalist in exile*

GIUSEPPE MAZZINI, *an Italian nationalist*

LAJOS KOSSUTH, *a Hungarian nationalist leader in exile*

CAPTAIN PEKS, *aide to Kossuth*

ALPHONSE DE VILLE, *aide to Ledru-Rollin*

PARLOURMAID

ZENKOWICZ, *a Polish émigré*

EMILY JONES, *Jones's wife*

CIERNECKI, *a Polish printer*

TCHORZEWSKI, *a Polish bookshop owner*

MICHAEL BAKUNIN, *a Russian anarchist in exile*

NICHOLAS OGAREV, *poet and co-editor of the* Bell

NATALIE OGAREV, *his wife*

MRS BLAINEY, *the Herzens' nanny*

A POLISH ÉMIGRÉ

IVAN TURGENEV, *a Russian novelist*

MARY SUTHERLAND, *Ogarev's mistress*

HENRY SUTHERLAND, *Mary's son*

NICHOLAS CHERNYSHEVSKY, *a Russian radical editor*

DOCTOR, *a nihilist*

PEROTKIN, *a visitor from Russia*

SEMLOV, *a visitor from Russia*

KORF, *a Russian officer*

PAVEL VETOSHNIKOV, *a visitor from Russia*

SLEPTSOV, *a Russian revolutionary*

LIZA, *Alexander and Natalie's daughter*

TERESINA, *Sasha's wife*

The action takes place between 1853 and 1865
in London and Geneva

Salvage

ACT ONE

London. The Herzen house in Hampstead. ALEXANDER
HERZEN, *aged forty, is asleep in an armchair, attended by dreams.
The room is (at this first appearance) without boundaries. The space
will remain loosely defined, serving for different rooms and changes of
address, and sometimes, as now, for exteriors.*

There is a wind blowing. Birdsong.

SASHA HERZEN, *aged thirteen, runs backwards across the stage
pulling on a kite string. He is accompanied by a young nurse (nanny),*
MARIA FOMM, *who is in charge of* TATA HERZEN, *aged
eight, and of a stroller or simple pram in which a two-year-old*
(OLGA) *is asleep. Speech is without accent except when inside
quotation marks. Herzen speaks from his chair.*

MARIA   Bring it down now, it's time to go home!

SASHA   No, isn't, it isn't!

MARIA (*as Sasha leaves*)   I'll tell your father!

HERZEN   Can you see, Tata? . . . the Cathedral of St Paul . . .
the Parliament House . . .

TATA   I know why it's called the Parliament House, Papa . . .
because you can see it from Parliament Hill.

Sasha returns, loudly aggrieved, winding his broken kite string.

SASHA   It broke!

MARIA   Don't wake Olga . . .

1

TATA Look!—there it goes! It's much higher than all the other kites, Sasha!

SASHA Well, of course it is—the string broke!

MARIA (*looking in the pram*) She's dropped a glove, we'll have to go back and look . . .

HERZEN We'll make another one, Sasha . . .

SASHA At once, please, Papa, will you?

MARIA Oh, look, it's in my pocket!

HERZEN If we stay here, you know, we'll have to learn to speak Eyseyki language.

SASHA 'I say, I say!'

HERZEN (*correcting, drawls*) 'I say, I say!'

Sasha follows Maria, Tata and Olga out.

SASHA (*leaving, mimicking*) 'I say, I say!'

In Herzen's dream, a number of people are taking the air on Parliament Hill. They are émigrés, political refugees, from Germany, France, Poland, Italy and Hungary.

The Germans: GOTTFRIED KINKEL (*thirty-seven*), *a tall, greying poet with a Jove-like head attached incongruously to a fastidious professor. He is his greatest admirer, but his handsome wife,* JOANNA (*thirty-two*), *runs him close.* MALWIDA VON MEYSENBUG (*thirty-six*), *their friend, is plain, intelligent, unmarried, romantic.* ARNOLD RUGE (*fifty*) *is a failed radical journalist, embittered and self-important.* KARL MARX *is thirty-four. His companion, the exception, is an Englishman,* ERNEST JONES (*thirty-three*), *a prominent Chartist of the middle classes.*

The French: ALEXANDRE LEDRU-ROLLIN (*forty-five*), *a large man, the leader of the 'official' (bourgeois) Republicans-in-exile;*

he is accompanied by an Aide. LOUIS BLANC (*forty-one*) *is a small man, the leader of the socialist faction of the Republicans-in-exile.*

The Pole is COUNT STANISLAW WORCELL (*fifty-three*), *a radicalised aristocrat, a gentle soul suffering from asthma.*

The Italian is the famous revolutionary GUISEPPE MAZZINI (*forty-seven*).

The Hungarian is LAJOS KOSSUTH (*fifty-one*), *the hero of his country's revolution, a handsome leader-in-exile. His Aide wears semi-military uniform.*

The Kinkels and Malwida are the first to appear.

JOANNA Dearest heart, are we wearing our special waistcoat? I'm simply terrified you'll catch a chill!

KINKEL Light of my life, the chills reel back in confusion from our special waistcoat.

JOANNA I've given Gottfried a life preserver, you know.

MALWIDA Is it flannel?

JOANNA There are dangers lying in wait for the unwary— including some of the female variety!

MALWIDA I'm a firm believer in flannel, myself.

JOANNA Don't scream when he pulls it out. Let Malwida have a look, my dearest.

Meanwhile, Kossuth and Ledru-Rollin have entered separately with their Aides. Each pair consults for a moment.

Joanna helps Kinkel to unbutton his coat. Malwida gives a little squeal.

MALWIDA Oh! Can I hold it?

The 'life preserver,' a revolver, is flourished by Kinkel. The two
AIDES, HUNGARIAN AND FRENCH, *approach each other,*
while Kossuth and Ledru-Rollin occupy themselves with the view.

HUNGARIAN AIDE (*clicking his heels*)   Captain Peks, aide-
de-camp to Monsieur le Gouverneur Kossuth.

FRENCH AIDE (*bowing*)   Enchanted. Alphonse de Ville, chief
secretary to Monsieur Ledru-Rollin.

HUNGARIAN AIDE   It is a great sorrow that two such heroes of
the revolutions in Europe have never met.

FRENCH AIDE   A tragedy.

HUNGARIAN AIDE   Inexplicable. Were Monsieur Ledru-Rollin
to find himself in Notting Hill on a Wednesday afternoon
between three and six o'clock, I assure you Monsieur le
Gouverneur would extend the hand of cordiality.

FRENCH AIDE   I thank you. But it is customary for calls to be
made by the *newer* arrivals on those already in residence.
Perhaps you know Parsons Green.

HUNGARIAN AIDE   It is true that Ledru-Rollin was here first,
but Kossuth, in the glorious period of the revolution, was
ruler of Hungary.

FRENCH AIDE (*agrees*)   Hungary. But Ledru-Rollin was a
minister in the government of the Second French Republic.

HUNGARIAN AIDE (*agrees*)   A minister.

FRENCH AIDE (*shrugs*)   So be it.

HUNGARIAN AIDE (*shrugs*)   Alas.

Mazzini, entering, greets Kossuth warmly, just as Jones,
accompanying Marx, enters and sees Ledru-Rollin.

MAZZINI Kossuth!—*Carissimo!*

JONES I say!—Ledru-Rollin! And Governor Kossuth! I say!

MAZZINI (*noticing Ledru-Rollin*) *Ministre! Bravissimo!*
(*introducing*) You know Kossuth . . .

JONES (*simultaneously to Kossuth*) You know Ledru-Rollin?

Kossuth and Ledru-Rollin recognise each other with incredulity and rapture.

LEDRU-ROLLIN Allow me to embrace you! France greets the hero of that great nation, Hungary!

KOSSUTH Your noble character, your courage, your sacrifice will be remembered wherever the torch of freedom burns!

LEDRU-ROLLIN The name of Kossuth will be immortal in the annals of the revolution in Europe!

KINKEL (*to Joanna and Malwida*) Don't look—it's that blackguard Marx.

MARX (*to Jones*) So you're still keeping in with that great flatulent bag of festering tripe Ledru-Rollin?

JONES Oh, I say!

MARX Kossuth doesn't know when history's scraped him off its shoe. As for Mazzini, the boil on my arse is more use than an Italian nationalist.

KINKEL (*to Joanna and Malwida*) Marx is always getting thrown out of pubs by the English workingman, what a charlatan!

All insults are spoken so as not to be audible to the insulted. Marx and Kinkel catch each other's eye.

MARX Kinkel! . . . Unctuous jackass.

5

Ruge enters.

MARX (*cont.*)   And here's another impudent windbag. Whenever I see Ruge, I think of those signs at certain street corners in Paris—'It is permitted to pass water here.'

RUGE (*greeting Ledru-Rollin and Kossuth*)   Monsieur le Ministre! Monsieur le Gouverneur! Who cracked first? I see my countryman over there, that swindler Marx. Oh, and Gottfried Kinkel—well, he's just a long streak of piss. So, when's the revolution?

LEDRU-ROLLIN   But for a miserable hundred thousand francs, I could give the signal for revolution in Paris tomorrow, or Tuesday at the latest.

MAZZINI   Paris—the whole of mankind, for that matter—will be liberated from Milano! My agents are in place.

Worcell and Blanc enter.

WORCELL (*coughing asthmatically*)   Poland greets Hungary, Italy and France!

BLANC   Socialist France greets Hungary, Italy and the bourgeois Republic-in-exile! . . . and Germany, Germany and Germany, 'Divided we fall, united we're fucked!'

Ruge and Kinkel cut each other. Ruge cuts Marx.

MARX (*to Jones*)   Watch out for that preening glove-puppet Louis Blanc—a deviationist to his stinking arsehole.

WORCELL (*shaking hands*)   Herzen! Poland forgives Russia!

JONES   I say! It's Herzen!

MARX   Russia is irrelevant. I propose Herzen is expelled from the Committee.

JONES   Oh, I say—that's simply not on.

MARX I resign!

Marx leaves. The émigrés watch him go, overtly catcalling now.

RUGE Abortionist!

KINKEL Parasite! Sponger!

LEDRU-ROLLIN Onanist!

MAZZINI Economist! (*generally*) *Arrivederci!* Today Milano—
tomorrow the world! (*Mazzini leaves.*)

BLANC Fantasist!

WORCELL (*to Jones*) Can we get on? I have to give a math
lesson in Muswell Hill at five o'clock.

JONES Gentlemen! Order, order! The European Committee
of Co-operation and Joint Action by the International
Brotherhood of Democrats in Exile is now in session!

*Unadvertised, a localised drama involving the Kinkels and Malwida
reaches an operatic climax, ignored by everyone else, with Joanna
waving the pistol at Kinkel and Malwida.*

JOANNA Do up your buttons! I was blind, blind!

*Joanna fires the pistol. The noise, like a slammed door, startles
Herzen awake.*

*The 'Herzen interior' from now on incorporates, permanently or
otherwise and according to needs, tables, chairs, armchairs, desk, couch
and so on, as well as notional doors and enclosed spaces.*

Malwida has just entered the room where Herzen has been asleep.

*The remaining members of the dream are 'next door' chatting socially,
holding glasses of wine, smoking, eating snacks replenished by a*
PARLOURMAID.

7

HERZEN (*waking*)   Oh! . . . Are you all right?

There is a burst of jovial laughter from the émigrés responding to some remark.

MALWIDA   I'm so sorry, the wind caught the door . . . I did knock.

HERZEN (*getting up*)   No—no—forgive me! I felt tired for a moment . . . and the next thing I knew . . .

MALWIDA   Were you having a dream?

HERZEN   My God, I hope so.

MALWIDA   I received your letter.

HERZEN   That's it. My letter.

MALWIDA   You want a tutor for your children.

HERZEN   Only for Tata. Sasha has his own tutors, and Olga is not old enough yet. The girls have been living with friends in Paris since my wife died, it's time I brought us all together again. Tata will need mathematics, history, geography . . . you have some English?

MALWIDA   I could teach a beginner. Would I be teaching in French or in German?

HERZEN   Undoubtedly!—We speak Russian *en famille*.

MALWIDA   I'd like to learn Russian. I've read *From the Other Shore*, but only in German, of course.

HERZEN   You know my book?

MALWIDA   At home I was close to someone who took part in the revolution. He died last year. He died young.

HERZEN   We are both bereaved.

MALWIDA   Somebody's lost a glove. A child . . .

Malwida picks up a small-sized glove from the floor by Herzen's chair. She gives him the glove. Herzen puts it in his pocket.

HERZEN   Yes, it's mine. Well—how much will I pay you?

MALWIDA   I would like to suggest two shillings an hour.

HERZEN   I would like to suggest three. Should we shake hands on it like Englishmen?

They shake hands. He starts escorting her to the other room.

HERZEN (*cont.*)   At home we used to call Englishmen 'Eyseyki'—'I say-ki!'

Malwida joins the Kinkels. Joanna is buttoning Kinkel's coat. Kossuth is making a round of farewell handshakes. The party is breaking up, assisted as appropriately by the Parlourmaid helping with coats and hats.

JOANNA   It is foggy out? My foolish cavalier is determined to provoke the Grim Reaper into an indiscretion!

HUNGARIAN AIDE (*to Herzen*)   Monsieur le Gouverneur begs to take his leave, that your guests may feel free to depart.

RUGE (*in 'English'*)   'Mr Jones—Marx tells me you Chartists will be the government in two years—and private property abolished in three!'

JONES   Oh, I say—I think that's premature.

LEDRU-ROLLIN   The revolution can only radiate from France! France means Europe! (*complaining to his Aide*) Look at that!—Kossuth is leaving before me!

KOSSUTH (*to Worcell*)   That admirable man Ledru-Rollin has his head in the clouds, I'm afraid.

WORCELL You heard? Mazzini is alive but in hiding.

KOSSUTH A brave patriot but, alas, a romantic.

Kossuth and Worcell shake hands. Kossuth shakes hands with Herzen and leaves.

KINKEL (*saying goodbye to Jones*) 'You show the steep and thorny way to heaven while we the Primrose Hill of dalliance tread.'

JONES (*baffled*) Indeed.

LEDRU-ROLLIN (*to his Aide*) And now those Germans! You'd better fetch a cab or I'll be last.

The Aide leaves on his errand.

KINKEL (*to Herzen*) Malwida showed me your letter, and I must tell you I was horrified. Letters in England must be folded in *three*—never in quarters! Especially when writing to a lady!

HERZEN (*to Malwida*) The children will be arriving with their nurse. She's a German girl, so you'll get on.

JOANNA We must go, we must go! Gottfried is losing his voice, and where will Germany be then?

Kinkel, Joanna and Malwida leave.

JONES (*to Herzen*) I promised Emily an early start on the compost.

HERZEN (*politely baffled*) 'Safe journey!'

Jones leaves. Herzen returns to the remaining guests—Blanc, Ledru-Rollin, Ruge and Worcell, who has fallen asleep.

LEDRU-ROLLIN (*to Blanc*) But, you know, when Kossuth's triumphal progress reached Marseilles, he talked socialism to the workers, and when he got to England, he praised parliamentary democracy!

HERZEN   Well, he would have been a fool to do it the other way round.

LEDRU-ROLLIN   But that's hypocrisy.

HERZEN   What is? To allow that here is not there? Cutting people out like pastry with your one true pastry-cutter makes you no better than the tyranny you're fighting.

BLANC   What's this?

HERZEN   It's all right . . . I had a dream about exiles. What a snake pit, adders' tongues weren't in it. But they spoke Russian! Extraordinary. You don't know Russian, do you?

BLANC (*put out*)   Why? Was I . . . ?

HERZEN   It was a dream. You wouldn't like it if you'd been left out. And it's true, anyway. The only thing that unites the émigrés is criticising the English. Blanc hates the English because they don't speak French.

BLANC   *Moi?*

HERZEN   You become furious when they don't know the way to Sharring Crow and Backay Strit.

LEDRU-ROLLIN   Not that the English aren't in some respects capable of improvement . . . The *slavery* of restaurants closed on Sundays. Is it some kind of restaurant-based theology? And when they're open, you want them closed as quickly as humanely possible . . .

BLANC   They have the ridiculous idea that they're the most advanced nation on earth, but they haven't discovered the principle of organisation. Everything here is connected in some incomprehensible sideways manner, instead of top to bottom like in a sensible country. There's no system to anything—society, the law, literary life—everything's just left to grow tangled together. There's a word here, 'shroobbery,' do you know it? I saw a sign at Keff Gardens, 'The Shroobbery', and there was nothing you could call a *garden* to be seen! England is one enormous shroobbery.

HERZEN   Keff Garden?

RUGE (*jeers*)   Not Keff! *Kev!*

BLANC (*irritated*)   Yes, Keff Gardens, they're famous. You ought to get out more instead of brooding over your Russian soul.

HERZEN   It's true—I haven't entered into English life. The English take us up with cries of interest and delight as if they've discovered a new amusement, like an acrobat or a singer, but it's a noise, an energy, to cover their instinctive aversion to foreigners. We're amusing when we wear a hat we brought from home, and even funnier when we put on a hat we bought in St James's. There's no way round it. But their coarseness is the sinew of some kind of brute confidence, which is the reason England is home to every shade of political exile. They don't give us asylum out of respect for the asylum-seekers but out of respect for themselves. They invented personal liberty, and they know it, and they did it without having any theories about it. They value liberty because it's liberty. So French history empties out through the Dover customs. King Louis-Philippe ran straight for the Channel, under the thoughtful pseudonym of 'Mr Smith' . . . and when the Republic took three lurches to the right, he was followed in order by the communist Barbès, the socialist Blanc, and the bourgeois republican Ledru-Rollin.

Ledru-Rollin's Aide enters with his master's coat.

FRENCH AIDE Your carriage awaits, Minister.

LEDRU-ROLLIN Ah, well. I part reluctantly from your comfortable and elegant house where we might have continued to discuss bourgeois republicanism . . .

RUGE I'll come with you. Good night, Herzen.

LEDRU-ROLLIN (*displeased*) But where do you live?

RUGE Brighton.

LEDRU-ROLLIN Brighton?!

RUGE Good night, Blanc.

While Ledru-Rollin is helped into his coat, Ruge goes out.

HERZEN He'll sleep on a bench at the station. (*Herzen tactfully shepherds Ledru-Rollin to the door.*) For the sake of the old days in Paris, eh?

LEDRU-ROLLIN (*grumbling*) Oh yes, I remember Ruge in the forties, fancying himself the leader of an international revolutionary movement, hanging around with Marx and Herwegh . . .

HERZEN (*sharply*) Let me see you out.

Herzen leaves with Ledru-Rollin and the Aide.

BLANC (*to Worcell*) Oh—oh! Did you hear that? We don't mention Herwegh! Are you asleep?

WORCELL (*waking*) What?

BLANC That ass Ledru-Rollin mentioned Herwegh . . . (*He uses his index fingers to make cuckold's horns.*) Herzen's wife and Herwegh, you know . . .

WORCELL (*shortly*)   What of it?

BLANC   Ah, yes—you're right. What of it?

Herzen returns.

BLANC (*cont.*)   Did you hear that poor Ruge announced a public lecture on German philosophy, and only two people turned up?

HERZEN   I was one of them.

WORCELL   And I was the other.

Herzen is near tears. He wipes his eyes covertly.

HERZEN   Ruge was someone to meet, when I was young in Moscow. We studied contraband copies of his newspaper like religious texts. When I read Bakunin in Ruge's *Deutsche Jahrbucher,* I thought, 'Yes, this is the language of free men! We'll make the revolution in Berlin, Paris, Brussels!' And the revolution when it came might have swept Ruge high up into the company of vindicated prophets . . . But the wave broke, and washed him up on the English shore, a refugee in the flotsam of refugees, their moment missed, their clothes shabbier by the month, their hopes shabbier, too . . . forever going over the past, living on recrimination and fantasy, schemers, dreamers, monomaniacs from every failed insurrection from Sicily to the Baltic, men who can't get their shoes mended sending agents with earth-shaking instructions to Marseilles, Lisbon, Cologne . . . men who walk across London to give a piano lesson redrawing the frontiers of Europe on the oilskin table-tops of back-street restaurants, toppling emperors like so many sauce bottles . . . and Marx in his proud retreat in the British Museum, anathemising everyone else . . . The clock has stopped in this theatre of political exile! You want to start it again at the moment when all was lost, so that you can make the same mistakes again. You reject the logic of why things went the way they did. That's vanity and cowardice.

BLANC Your language is extravagant. I ignore it because it's the language of a bystander. Your father left you rich, and you have been generous, but you're a tourist and occasional journalist. Worcell, for example, leads the cause of Polish independence from his basement room in Hunter Street and gives mathematics lessons to earn a few shillings, but he is a revolutionary. Good night, gentlemen. (*Blanc leaves.*)

WORCELL (*deflecting*) Don't.

HERZEN I wasn't going to. (*Pause.*) Independence isn't all it's cracked up to be, you know.

Worcell laughs asthmatically.

HERZEN (*cont.*) What country could be more independent than Russia? And in Russia now there isn't a squeak or a pinpoint of light. I have nowhere to publish. The *Contemporary* has stuck its head up out of harm's way. And to whom would I speak? About what? I've stopped quarrelling with the world. (*Worcell laughs.*) No, I really have. I sat in this chair the first morning I woke up in this house. I'd just arrived in England, and for the first time . . . for the first time since Natalie died . . . no, from before that, I don't know since when . . . but for the first time in a long time, there was silence. I didn't have to talk or think or move, nothing was expected of me, I knew nobody and nobody knew where I was, everything was behind me, all the moving from place to place, the quarrels and celebrations, the desperate concerns of health and happiness, love, death, printer's errors, picnics

ruined by rain, the endless tumult of ordinary life . . . and I
just sat quiet and alone all that day, looking at the tops of the
trees on Primrose Hill through the mist. It was as if I'd come
to the end of a long journey that started when I left Moscow
more than six years ago with Natalie and the children and my
mother, packed into a carriage hung with furs against the
January cold. Half a dozen sledges with our friends came to
see us off as far as the staging post, and then we were on our
way to a land of limitless possibilities, known intimately from
our dreams. I came to Paris as people used to come to
Jerusalem or Rome, and found the city of the plain. It made
one half-hearted effort to be worthy of itself and then
collapsed satisfied under six feet of dung, not even brimstone.
I have lost every illusion dear to me. I'm forty. I will dwell
in the land of Nod, to the east of Eden, and the world will
hear no more of me.

WORCELL   I came to speak to you . . . about . . . to ask you to
help us . . . to start a Polish press in London.

HERZEN   A free Polish press? Yes. You should. You should.
It's a good idea. Isn't there a Pole—yes—

WORCELL   Tchorzewski—

HERZEN   (*simultaneously*)—Tchorzewski who keeps a bookshop
in Soho? Not only that, you've got people coming and
going all the time, you could get material from home and
smuggle in real news and discussion—wake up the
intelligentsia, educate the young people, bring fresh blood
to the cause. I'll write something for you—you can translate
it. Better still . . . can you get hold of Cyrillic type?

WORCELL   (*nods*)   From Paris . . . We can buy second-hand fonts.

HERZEN   (*galvanised*)   A free Russian press!—and Polish. Do
you know a printer?

WORCELL Ciernecki is a printer.

HERZEN We'll need—

WORCELL Premises.

HERZEN (*simultaneously*)—premises. Have a seat!
(*Herzen sits down and grabs a sheet of paper and a pen.*)
We'll need a supplier, paper, ink, an assistant, part-time to
begin with . . . what else? How much?

FEBRUARY 1853

'The Schoolroom.'

*A table with a cloth reaching the floor. Malwida enters, holding the
necessities of giving a lesson, but in mid-pantomime in search of a lost
child whom she knows to be hiding under the table.*

MALWIDA Now, where could she have got to! I'm sure I saw
her come in here! What a mystery! Oh, dear, perhaps she's
lost forever!

*And so on, with sounds of excited suppressed delight emanating from
under the table, until, after drawing a blank here and there, Malwida
peeks under the tablecloth, releasing a paroxysm of pleasure from the
unseen Olga.*

Tata enters with her schoolbooks.

MAY 1853

*A party can be heard going on, with laughter and some music and
singing in Russian. Herzen and Worcell, with drinks in hand, study
printed Cyrillic sheets. Maria enters, complaining.*

MARIA   *Sascha muss ins Bett. Er hoert nicht auf mich!—und jetzt ist auch noch Tata heruntergekommen!* [Sasha has to go to bed. I have no control over him!—and now Tata has come downstairs!]

Herzen waves her away without looking up. Maria leaves.

WORCELL   To read such things, printed in Russian . . . it makes you frightened.

Sasha enters, complaining.

SASHA   *Papa—Herr Ciernecki zeigt mir gerade—*[Papa— Mr Ciernecki is showing me—]

HERZEN   Am I a German?

SASHA   Maria says I have to go to bed, and Mr Ciernecki is teaching me chords!

HERZEN   Come here. Come close. Look at this.

Sasha takes the sheet.

SASHA   What does it say?

HERZEN   You can read it.

SASHA   It's difficult.

HERZEN   Difficult? What is that tutor reading with you?

SASHA   Marlinski's stories, they're exciting.

HERZEN   Well, just read the words at the top, about the crow.

SASHA   Why?

HERZEN   It's an article by your papa.

SASHA   'I am not yet the real crow but only a small crow . . . the real one is still flying in the sky . . .'

HERZEN The words of Pugachev, who made a rebellion against the Tsarina Katerina in the eighteenth century. Now this is why you must remember today. What I have written—words like these—have rarely been whispered at home, even more rarely written down, but in the whole history of Russia they have never before been in print. *This is the first time.* Will you remember?

Sasha nods.

SASHA Will you come and hear me play?

Herzen cuffs Sasha affectionately. He picks up his glass. Worcell does the same.

HERZEN To the Free Russian and Polish Press in London.

They drain their glasses and smash them joyfully, embrace and leave, Sasha with them.

SEPTEMBER 1853

The Schoolroom. Malwida and Tata are at the table, Tata having an English lesson, reading hesitantly aloud.

TATA 'Georges and Marie go . . .'

MALWIDA 'George and Mary.'

TATA 'George and Mary go to the . . .'

MALWIDA 'Seaside.'

TATA 'One day in Augoost.'

MALWIDA Good.

TATA 'One day in Augoost, Mrs Brown said to George . . .' (*Tata yawns.*)

MALWIDA Are you tired this morning, Tata?

TATA Yes, Miss Malwida. I could hardly get out of bed.

MALWIDA Hm. Is that why you haven't brushed your hair?

TATA I brushed it.

MALWIDA Fifty strokes of the brush with each hand, that's what I was taught. However . . . Go on, please.

TATA 'Said to George, Marie, Mary, cannot go on holiday with her family because they are poor . . .'

Maria enters hot and bothered, holding a toddler's shoe.

MARIA *Ist Olga hier?* [Is Olga here?]

MALWIDA *Olga? Nein, leider nicht, Maria.* [Olga? No, I'm afraid not, Maria.]

Maria makes a bad-tempered sound and leaves.

TATA She'll be in the kitchen after a liquorice from cook, you'll see.

Tata returns to the book. Malwida, nervous, looks quickly under the table.

MALWIDA Continue.

TATA 'Said to George, Marie, Mary, cannot go on holiday with her family because they are poor . . .' Where will you go for *your* holiday, Miss Malwida?

MALWIDA To Broadstairs. Perhaps . . . (*panicking*) We must all help to look for Olga.

Piano 'music' is heard, the keys hit randomly.

TATA (*laughs*) It's Olga. Miss Malwida, which do you think is greater—England or Germany?

MALWIDA Back to George and Mary. However, at Lord Wellington's funeral they played Beethoven's 'Funeral March.' I think that's all that needs to be said.

The 'Olga piano' ceases, Maria is heard scolding her.

TATA Can we do piano now?

MALWIDA I think we might stick to the timetable.

Olga is smacked and gives out howls.

MALWIDA (*cont.*) (*cross*) Oh, really!

Malwida leaves, Tata gathers up her books and skips after her.

NOVEMBER 1853

Herzen enters triumphantly, spinning a half-sovereign. Sasha follows, carrying a ruptured parcel of stacked pamphlets, several pounds in weight.

SASHA Where shall I put them?

HERZEN Half a sovereign! Cash! Tchorzewski has taken ten copies! (*He empties a cigar box and puts the coin in it. He rattles the box.*) Our first earnings.

Sasha dumps the parcel on the table.

SASHA How many are there left?

HERZEN Four hundred and ninety. They're going like hot biscuits. Give this shilling to the boy.

SASHA A shilling!

Leaving, he is met by Malwida, unusually emotional.

MALWIDA Sasha, Sasha, are you well? Did you miss me? Where are the girls?

HERZEN Miss von Meysenbug . . . Go on, Sasha, he's waiting.

Sasha leaves.

HERZEN (*cont.*) You've returned early? Has something happened? Sit down . . . please . . . There. You didn't like Broadstairs?

MALWIDA It wasn't that. You received my letter?

HERZEN Of course. But was it a serious suggestion?—to send the children?

MALWIDA I missed them so much! I thought you might—

HERZEN Too busy! And Maria's English puts Broadstairs out of range, she can hardly get to town and back without a misadventure, lost omnibus tickets, parcels, children . . .

MALWIDA It's not Maria's fault she can't manage . . . I have come with a proposal . . . that I should live in the house and take charge of the children—I mean their physical and moral welfare, their general deportment, to be a companion and guide, to preserve the children for their father and the father for his children. Maria, of course, will carry on in those areas suited to her, the laundry, the pantry, and so on—

Herzen makes to interrupt.

MALWIDA (*cont.*) I must only add that since the offer is made out of friendship, I would accept no payment, other than for those lessons I would continue to give.

Herzen takes both her hands.

HERZEN Miss von Meysenbug . . . welcome to my house. Welcome! My mother was German, you know.

MALWIDA Was she?

HERZEN   I'm half German! Luckily, the bottom half. Let's go and find the children. When would you like to move in? Tomorrow?

MALWIDA (*dubiously*)   Oh . . .

HERZEN   Today?

MALWIDA (*laughs*)   No! The beginning of the week, shall we say? But it's better if you explain to the children, and to Maria . . .

HERZEN   You're right.

MALWIDA   I must go home now.

HERZEN   Of course.

They shake hands.

MALWIDA   By the way . . . I myself am half French.

HERZEN   I might have guessed. *À bientôt!*

MALWIDA   *Kharashó. Da svidániya.* [Yes—goodbye.]

HERZEN (*delighted*)   *Da svidániya!* [Goodbye!]

Herzen shows her out.

JANUARY 1854

Sasha and Tata, strikingly spruced up, Tata with white cuffs, enter and stand side by side in readiness for an inspection . . . while a table, set for six, is laid with breakfast by the Parlourmaid. Malwida enters briskly.

MALWIDA   *Dóbroye óotra, dyéti!* [Good morning, children!]

SASHA AND TATA   *Dóbroye óotra*, Miss Malwida. [Good morning, Miss Malwida!]

Sasha and Tata present both sides of their hands for inspection. Malwida then scrutinises their ears.

MALWIDA   *Prekrásna!* . . . *A ty samá* . . . [Excellent! . . . Did you choose . . .] . . . (*abandoning Russian*) Did you choose your blouse this morning, Tata?

TATA   No, Miss Malwida.

MALWIDA   Well, let's go in to breakfast, shall we?

Sasha draws Malwida's chair back for her. Malwida sits. Sasha, with a smirk, draws a chair back for Tata. Tata, with a pleased smirk, sits. Sasha sits. Malwida's place is next to Herzen's. The empty chair (Olga's) is next. Tata and Sasha sit opposite, with Maria at the foot of the table opposite Herzen's place.

MALWIDA (*cont.*)   Hands!

Tata removes her wrists from the table and puts them in her lap.

Maria enters. Sasha stands and draws her chair back. Maria pulls her chair out of Sasha's hands and sits glowering.

MALWIDA (*cont.*)   Maria—if you would be so good—Tata's blouse is not suitable for school mornings. White cuffs pick up every little smut and look grubby for the rest of the day. The blouse with the grey cuffs would be preferable.

MARIA   It's in the wash.

MALWIDA (*politely surprised*)   *Still?* Hm . . . !

MARIA   And may I say—

Herzen enters with a newspaper.

CHILDREN   *Dóbroye óotra, Papá!* [Good morning, Papa!]

MALWIDA   *Dóbroye óotra!* [Good morning!]

HERZEN   *Dóbroye óotra!* [Good morning!]

Herzen sits down. Malwida pours coffee for him and for Maria. The children have pre-poured glasses of milk. Malwida has her own teapot. At Malwida's nod, the children drink from their glasses. Breakfast is a cold collation. Herzen and Maria help themselves, Malwida takes nothing but helps the children.

Sasha, undetected for the moment, opens a book.

HERZEN *(to Maria)*   Where's Olga?

MALWIDA   We had our breakfast early. *(She notices Tata pouring herself coffee.)* Tata . . . !

TATA   Maria said I could.

MARIA   Coffee in the morning keeps a body regular.

MALWIDA   And excitable.

She removes Tata's coffee cup away from her. Maria gets up and flounces out. Malwida takes no notice. She sees Sasha's book.

MALWIDA *(cont.)*   Reading at table? What will your father think of me?

SASHA   I'm not reading, I have to learn it.

HERZEN   Homework? There's a time for homework.

SASHA   Well, I couldn't, could I? I was doing your envelopes!

HERZEN   What about later?

SASHA   I would have missed the fun later.

HERZEN *(making an effort)*   Well, you have to choose between homework and breakfast!

Sasha jumps up and hurries out with his nose in the book.

HERZEN (*cont.*)   Yes, I'm posting fifty copies to the enemy's citadels. Free subscriptions for the Winter Palace . . . the Ministry of the Interior, the censorship office, the Third Section, the police . . .

MALWIDA   If you don't want any breakfast, you'd better leave the table, Tata.

TATA   Thank you, Miss Malwida. (*Tata takes the hint and leaves.*)

HERZEN   Maria has a good heart, I know you can come to an understanding with her. She has been with the children since Natalie died, Olga remembers no one else.

MALWIDA   My only concern is to give them a happy, well-ordered childhood.

HERZEN   And you are succeeding. You know that a German once did a great evil in my life . . . which you, in your way, are making good.

MALWIDA   Then please let me tell you frankly, Alexander, that you're not helping me by keeping open house for the émigré population of London. Almost every day and into the night, these people, some of them no better than riff-raff, disturb the family peace, battening on you for free food, drink and entertainment . . .

HERZEN   Oh . . . But how . . . ?

MALWIDA   My advice is to set aside two evenings a week to receive your acquaintances. On the other evenings, and during the daytime—

HERZEN   By invitation only—easily done! You're right!

MALWIDA   Thank you. We're so . . . available here. If we lived a little further out . . .

HERZEN   The lease is almost up—where would you like to live?

MALWIDA   Oh . . . really! Well . . . Richmond, perhaps. The park would be lovely for the children, and it's on the railway . . .

HERZEN   That's settled, then.

PARLOURMAID (*entering*)   Worcell's come, he's got a tramp with him. And Maria's packing!

HERZEN   'Thank you.'

The Parlourmaid leaves.

HERZEN (*cont.*)   I'll talk to her.

MALWIDA   It's for the best, Alexander.

Malwida leaves, exchanging greetings with Worcell and another Pole of about the same age, ZENKOWICZ, as they enter.

HERZEN   Come in, come in, I was just finishing . . . there's coffee . . .

WORCELL   No—no—please. This is a melancholy business. Zenkowicz explained, our delegate is ready to leave for Poland. But the expense . . .

HERZEN (*to Zenkowicz*)   I told you I would give ten pounds.

ZENKOWICZ (*rudely*)   Ten pounds! That's a joke! He'll need sixty pounds at least, and we're forty short.

HERZEN   Well, this is very strange. He's your delegate, not mine. I was surprised to be asked at all.

ZENKOWICZ   He is taking Russian printed sheets.

HERZEN   Yes, he is. I pay for the press, the rent, the labour, paper, ink . . . You undertook to dispatch my

27

Russian sheets through your channels. That was our arrangement.

ZENKOWICZ   As though you didn't know we haven't a penny!

HERZEN   So, it seems we have divided our responsibilities with the condition that both halves fall on me.

ZENKOWICZ   There's no point in arguing over nothing— what do you want from us?

HERZEN   You have no right to demand my money like a brigand.

ZENKOWICZ   A brigand? I have the honour to be Chief of Staff to Count Worcell, whom you insult by—

WORCELL (*distressed*)   I cannot permit this conversation to continue. Herzen, you're right, but what can we do?

Sasha enters with his schoolbooks.

HERZEN (*to Zenkowicz*)   Come with me. (*to Worcell*) It's for your sake only and, on my word of honour, for the last time.

Herzen and Zenkowicz leave. Sasha and Worcell sit down at the table. The Maid enters and clears the table. Worcell puts on his spectacles. Sasha opens his books.

WORCELL   So. Have you done your homework?

31 DECEMBER 1854

The Herzen house, Richmond.

The table is overwhelmed . . . by a crowd of guests, by the remains of an elaborate buffet, by Christmas decorations. There are paper hats, there is

singing and shouting and drinking. Worcell is among the
guests. Herzen is in the crowd. Maria's replacement, an English nurse,
MRS BLAINEY, *brings Sasha and Tata. Also present are Kinkel,*
Joanna, Blanc, Jones, Mrs Jones (EMILY), CIERNECKI (*the*
Polish printer), TCHORZEWSKI (*of the bookshop*) *and other*
ÉMIGRÉS *male and female. Ciernecki is playing his guitar. There is*
part of a large Christmas tree visible. Sasha and Tata, a year older,
nearly two years since Parliament Hill, are dressed up for the occasion.
A home-made '1855' hangs like washing on a line, each child-written
digit on a separate sheet.

JONES (*raising his glass to Blanc*)   To victory for La Grande
Alliance in the Crimea!

EMILY   And one in the eye for Russia!

JONES (*noticing Herzen*)   Not to be taken personally!

WORCELL   You understand, *cher* Herzen, that I can't ask you
to speak at our meeting. We've put our cause under English
patronage, and it's impossible to explain to our friends in
Parliament that Herzen and England have a common enemy
in the Crimea.

HERZEN (*toasting*)   To England! I'll never get over this place.
In the street today there were urchins shouting for Prince
Albert to be sent to the Tower . . .

JONES (*chuckling*)   Ah yes, well, Prussia is taking an unhelpful
attitude to the Crimean business.

HERZEN (*seriously astonished*)   No, but really. *The Times*
reported a public meeting calling for the Queen of
England's husband to be *impeached*—and nobody is arrested!
Not even the editor!

JONES   Having one's say isn't grounds for arrest, why should
it be?

HERZEN   I don't know! It just feels so . . . *strange.*

KINKEL (*interrupting*)   So you won't be speaking at the 1848 anniversary?

HERZEN   Won't I? I thought I was. (*to Jones*) *Et tu, Brute?*

KINKEL   Oh! I've put my toe in it!

JONES   The fact is, Marx says he refuses to share a platform with you.

HERZEN   In that case, I'd like to accept your invitation to speak.

JONES   Quite right, quite right. (*Shouts.*) Ladies and gentlemen! Your attention please!

The noise reduces generally.

JONES (*cont.*)   Thank you! While so many of us are here . . . For your diaries—citizens—comrades—an International Soirée and Public Meeting to commemorate the Great Revolutionary Movement of 1848 . . . will be held at St Martin's Hall, Long Acre, on February 27th, that's a Tuesday, please note . . . Tea on table at five o'clock— thank you, ladies!—door to hall open seven-thirty for eight. On the platform: Messieurs, in alphabetical order, Barbès, Blanc, Cuningham, Cooper, Herzen, Hugo, Kinkel, Kossuth, Ledru-Rollin . . .

EMILY   The platform will collapse! *Le plate-forme* . . .

JONES   Ha-ha, Marx, no, not Marx, Mayne-Reid, Mazzini, we hope, Saffi and Worcell. Double tickets, two shillings and sixpence—single tickets, one shilling and sixpence— meeting only, threepence . . . Thank you!

TCHORZEWSKI   How much for tea only?

Jones 'stands down' amid laughter. Emily squeezes his hand. Blanc and Herzen catch each other's eye.

BLANC The rock against which the revolution breaks. There were eleven dead at Peterloo, eleven!—and they call it a 'massacre.'

Ciernecki comes to Herzen with a small book, wrapped.

CIERNECKI Herzen! It's come. It'll cost you the cab from the binders.

HERZEN Ciernecki!

He kisses Ciernecki and tears open the wrapper. He kisses the book . . . and shouts for silence.

HERZEN (*cont.*) Time! Who has the right time? Gottfried, what time is it?

GUESTS Plenty of time—at least five minutes! . . . Eleven fifty-eight . . . One minute to! . . . Four minutes to! . . . Exactly midnight . . . We've missed it! Two minutes past! (*etc.*)

Malwida succeeds in hushing everyone up. She has a reason: when all is quiet, distant church bells are heard.

BLANC (*putting away his watch*) Three minutes early.

But the others, now including the Parlourmaid, cheer, raise glasses, kiss each other, shake hands.

Into the midst of this, at waist level, Olga, aged four, appears in her nightdress, looking for Malwida—who swoops on her with endearments in German and carries her off to protests that Olga should remain. Herzen makes space and silence for himself. Malwida hands over Olga to the Nurse.

HERZEN I have something to give to my son, Sasha, and something to say to him.

Applause. Sasha is pushed, bashful, into prominent view.

HERZEN (*cont.*) Sasha . . . this is a book I wrote in the year of revolution, six years ago now. It was only ever published in German. But here it is at last in Russian, as I wrote it. I put into your hand this occasionally impudent protest against ideas which are obsolete and fraudulent, against absurd idols that belong to another age. Don't look for solutions in this book. There are none. Anything which is solved is over and done with. The coming revolution is the only religion I pass on to you, and it's a religion without a paradise on the other shore. But do not remain on this shore. Better to perish. Go in your time, preach the revolution at home to our own people. There they once loved my voice, and will perhaps remember me.

Herzen presents the book. There is applause. Sasha bursts into tears and hugs him. The party closes around them, applauding. Malwida is dabbing tears from her eyes.

HERZEN (*cont.*) (*Calls out.*) It's a beautiful frosty night, who's for greeting the New Year in Richmond Park?

There is assent and enthusiasm. Herzen notices that he's offended Blanc, who makes his own departure, obscured by the general exodus. The Maid begins to clear the table. Herzen and Sasha look up at the stars. The guests move away in groups in the darkness. Joanna is heard rather than seen—

JOANNA Dear heart, do you want to put your hand in my muff?

—followed by a suppressed shriek, laughter and shushing.

Tata, wearing a shawl, comes to Herzen with another.

TATA Papa . . .

Herzen puts the shawl on Sasha.

HERZEN I'm not cold at all. It's dry cold, like in Switzerland. You don't remember.

SASHA I do.

TATA Kolya was at the deaf school—I remember Switzerland.

Herzen collects the children into his embrace.

HERZEN It's good to be talking Russian together. We must always . . . Mummy was teaching Kolya Russian words, do you—?

TATA They're both dead, and that's all. Well, they are. We can't help it. (*She frees herself without fuss and goes away.*)

HERZEN You'd better go to bed, too.

He kisses Sasha, who follows Tata out. Herzen emits a private howl. He becomes aware of someone—MICHAEL BAKUNIN— standing a few paces behind him. He does not turn.

HERZEN (*cont.*) Who is . . . ? (*He turns.*) Oh! . . . Bakunin! . . . (*He gives a small embarrassed laugh.*) I thought it was Natalie.

BAKUNIN No, she's dead.

HERZEN How are you? I mean apart from . . .

BAKUNIN Well, you know. (*Pause.*) What is it?

HERZEN Oh, Michael . . . I want her back so that I can take her for granted again and be busy and full of sap putting idiots in their place. I'm surrounded by them.

BAKUNIN You always were.

HERZEN   No, that was friendly argument. Being proved wrong has made them cocky. They're more certain than ever that the people are natural republicans waiting to be led out of bondage. But the people are more interested in potatoes than freedom. The people think equality means everyone should be oppressed equally. They love authority. They're suspicious of talent. They want a government to govern for them and not against them. To govern themselves doesn't enter their heads. We thought we could educate the people like a horse doctor blowing a pill into a horse. We thought we could set the pace for social change. The emperors did more than keep their thrones, they pushed our faces into the wreck of our belief in the revolutionary instincts of the people.

BAKUNIN   A minor setback!

Herzen laughs.

BAKUNIN (*cont.*)   Reaction is only the optical effect of the river running backwards on the tide, while the river runs always to the sea, which is liberty boundless and indivisible!

HERZEN   Dear Michael! Dear irreplaceable friend. For as long as I've known you, your unquenchable spirit, your unwavering conviction, have filled me with the desire to smash you over the head with a—baguette.

BAKUNIN (*happily*)   You faintheart. You need me to remind you what it is to be free.

HERZEN   But you're in prison.

BAKUNIN   That's why you aren't free.

HERZEN   I'm dizzy.

BAKUNIN To be freedom, freedom must be freedom *for all*—for the equality of each!

HERZEN Stop . . . stop . . .

BAKUNIN It's within our grasp, Herzen, if we can only remove the fetters from humanity.

HERZEN I think you're saying we'd all be free if humanity were given its liberty.

BAKUNIN Yes!

HERZEN I was afraid of that.

BAKUNIN Left to themselves, people are noble, generous, uncorrupted, they'd create a completely new kind of society if only people weren't so blind, stupid and selfish.

HERZEN Is that the same people or different people?

BAKUNIN The same people.

HERZEN You're doing it on purpose.

BAKUNIN No—listen! Once—long ago, at the beginning of history—we were all free. Man was at one with his nature, and so he was good. He was in harmony with the world. Conflict was unknown. Then the serpent entered the garden, and the name of the serpent was—Order. Social organisation! The world was no longer at one with itself. Matter and spirit divided. Man was no longer whole. He was riven by ambition, acquisitiveness, jealousy, fear . . . Conflict became the condition of his life, the individual against his neighbour, against society, against himself. The Golden Age was ended. How can we make a new Golden Age and set men free again? By destroying everything that destroyed their freedom.

HERZEN (*nostalgically*) Ah, the zig and the zag.

BAKUNIN I knew you understood. The age has arrived at its reversal, and we were born to be the turning point. The year of revolution cracked the foundations of the old world. Things will never be the same again.

HERZEN (*exasperated*) Things *are* the same again! Reaction has triumphed, and the same idiots are making the same speeches, calling on people to sacrifice themselves for abstract nouns that have no connection with reality. Who is there brave enough to say that dying for liberty or progress is not the apex of human happiness when the sacrifice is for vainglory and five kinds of authority dressed up in revolutionary slogans? I offended Blanc just now. His version of utopia has come through without a scratch: the organisation of labour on the Ancient Egyptian model, without the Pharaoh's concern for personal liberties. It's going to have to be up to us.

BAKUNIN You, now.

HERZEN I mean Russia. The Russian people. (*vehemently*) Cutting myself off from home was the worst mistake of my life! The Tsar was going to be swept off the board by the tilt from . . . from what? Card-house republics? Bickering parliaments terrified equally of emperors and the masses? Constitutions and militias from Vienna to Berlin to put the fear of God into the Russian army? What fools we look now! Tsar Nicholas just tightened the screws—no more passports, no contact, no discussion, perpetual fear, lights out and no whispering! With the Free Russian Press I thought I could start people at home thinking again. I imagine Nick Ogarev reading me—I write everything for Nick—but I might as well put it in a bottle and throw it in the sea. I'm left stranded like the sole survivor of a disaster of my own making.

BAKUNIN   Not at all, not at all, this is just a hiccup! The Tsar could die tomorrow.

Herzen laughs. Tata is heard calling for him.

MARCH 1855

It is daytime. The area around the table erupts into celebration. 'Every Russian in London' and affiliated Poles and others are dancing and embracing as though it were New Year's Eve again. But the Christmas decorations have gone. Herzen tumbles in from the door with several new arrivals. He is showing 'everyone' a story in The Times.

Tata and Olga (still about four and a half) are dancing hand in hand and barefoot on the table amid glasses and bottles (perhaps). Tata is shouting, 'Papa! Papa!'

TATA   Papa—Papa—listen to Olga!

HERZEN   Yes—yes—come in—every Slav in London is already here—we're drunk—we're mad—we're young again!

TATA AND OLGA (*sing*)   'Zarnicol is dead! Zarnicol is dead! Hip-hooray and fiddle-di-dee, Zarnicol is dead!'

Olga is applauded and lifted down from the table by Malwida. Tata steps down using a chair.

MALWIDA (*to Tata*)   Feet off, feet off! (*to the Nurse*) Did she do her business?

TATA (*hurt*)   Ow!

Tata examines her bare foot.

The proceedings continue, noisily at first.

The Parlourmaid meanwhile re-sets the table, removing bottles and glasses and laying places, at the same time 'joining in.'

Worcell, physically overcome, settles in an armchair. He falls asleep as one of the guests and remains to awake in the next scene.

HERZEN   I met the new Tsar once, you know, when he was the Crown Prince and I was in exile in Vyatka.

SASHA   What was he like?

HERZEN   I liked him. A decent fellow.

MALWIDA   Did you meet his father too?

HERZEN   No, but I saw him once. His eyes were like pewter, I never looked into a colder face.

ÉMIGRÉ He's even colder now!

TATA (*to Malwida*)   I've got a splinter in my foot . . . Don't touch it, don't touch it!

MALWIDA   Who said I was going to touch it? . . . Oh yes, I can see it, it's sticking out. That's lucky. It's gone.

On the word, Malwida deftly removes the splinter. Tata yelps.

MALWIDA (*cont.*)   With pain, quick is best. No tears, please.

A song is taken up. The celebration disperses. Herzen ends up at his desk.

APRIL 1856

Evening.

The Parlourmaid completes setting the table and leaves. Herzen sorts papers, reads proofs, scribbles. He has a new periodical, the Polar Star. *Worcell sleeps. Malwida enters with Olga, who is dressed for bed. Herzen kisses Olga and they say good night in Russian ['Spakóynoy nóchi']. Malwida takes Olga out.*

Worcell's congested chest wakes him.

WORCELL   What?

HERZEN (*pauses to think*)   I said, 'Why don't you have a nap?'

WORCELL   Oh . . . no, no . . .

HERZEN   Letters, people travelling again—the universities wide open, censorship in retreat . . . I've had letters from young men who were children when I left home. I swear I wept.

Worcell looks about.

WORCELL   You've changed the furniture.

HERZEN   Yes, we moved house while you were asleep, we're in Finchley.

WORCELL   Of course, I remember. When I lived up in the world in Burton Crescent, a ground-floor terrace, I came home one day and found a man sitting by the fire. I said, 'Oh—I am afraid you have been waiting for me. How can I help you?' He said, 'Before I answer, may I know to whom I have the honour of speaking?' Then I noticed the furniture was different. A few days later the same thing happened again, only this time he was at the table eating supper with his wife. He simply raised his hand and said, 'No, you live at Number 43.' (*Pause.*) He was an Englishman. I wonder what Poles would be like if we had a navy.

Herzen comes to him and takes both his hands.

HERZEN   Worcell, come and live with me. I'll give you two rooms to yourself, you can breakfast alone, dine alone if you like, keep open hours for your people, sit in the garden . . .

WORCELL I should certainly live twice as long on the Finchley heights . . . but it's impossible. Our fellows are split and fractious, it would look as though I'd deserted them. I thank you with all my heart, but forgive me, Herzen, while Tsar Nicholas was alive, the Russian and Polish exiles had a common cause . . . Now, with the mood of reform . . .

HERZEN It's only the committee you surround yourself with who won't trust us.

WORCELL But it's far too late to alter that.

HERZEN Then let them shift for themselves. They're living off sacred relics and a history of glorious defeats—

WORCELL (*sharply*) It's when you speak like this that they, and I, too, find my affection for you ill-directed.

HERZEN Worcell, forgive me. Will you forgive me?

WORCELL No, not tonight.

Malwida enters. He nods a courteous farewell and moves to leave.

MALWIDA You're not staying?

WORCELL No—thank you.

MALWIDA Wait till I get your coat. It's chilly in the hall. (*Malwida leaves.*)

HERZEN All right, then, let me take a room for you at the Brompton Consumption Hospital for a few weeks while you're thinking about it—to set you right.

WORCELL I'm sure that would be an excellent thing, but it's a fearful distance for Szebicki to come with the daily report. It's impossible . . .

Malwida returns with his coat and helps him into it.

WORCELL (*cont.*) . . . and far too late. Thank you. I seem to be a glove short.

HERZEN A glove . . . ?

WORCELL No matter. Last time I had three. That probably explains it.

MALWIDA Are you walking home?

WORCELL It's all downhill.

Malwida shows Worcell out and returns. Herzen is looking at the Polar Star.

MALWIDA I've been trying to read your open letter to the Tsar, but it's too difficult for me.

HERZEN Malwida, I never took you seriously enough.

MALWIDA Oh?

HERZEN As a political exile.

MALWIDA Oh, really . . . (*Pause.*) Alexander . . . you're not wearing your wedding ring.

HERZEN I know—it broke! During the night. I found it in the bed, in two pieces.

MALWIDA It broke by itself?

HERZEN (*amused*) Are you superstitious?

The doorbell is heard as the Parlourmaid enters with a dish for the table.

PARLOURMAID It's people with luggage, I saw from the area—Sasha's gone.

Herzen hurries towards the sound of loud greetings.

HERZEN It's Ogarev's voice! *(offstage) Éto gólos Agaryóva!*
Nyevyerayátna! [I don't believe it!]

*The arrivals are OGAREV and NATALIE. The noise is
considerable, Natalie highly emotional, weeping over Sasha and Tata.
The scrum of five people with twice as many parcels, bundles, bags,
etc., explodes into the room, kissing and weeping, and exclaiming at
the length of the journey, the ages of the children, the changed
appearances . . .*

*Offstage, the language is Russian and on re-entry remains theoretically
in Russian.*

Malwida, who had remained motionless, rises to face the invasion.

NATALIE Where's Olga? I want to see Olga.

HERZEN This is the children's governess, Miss von
Meysenbug.

MALWIDA I'm quite pleased to meet you.

HERZEN She's learning Russian.

NATALIE *Enchantée.*

HERZEN Nick!

NATALIE I am Madame Ogarev. I was Natalie Herzen's best
friend.

HERZEN And Nick is mine.

NATALIE I was only nineteen and she was thirty, but we were
inseparable . . . before I went home and met this charming
gentleman here—I know we shall get on beautifully.

Malwida is uncomprehending. Ogarev greets her.

HERZEN (*ignored*)   *Parlez français* . . . [Speak French . . .]

MALWIDA   *Non—je vous en prie* . . . [No—please—I insist . . .]

NATALIE (*to Tata*)   You were no bigger than a mushroom.

SASHA   I remember you. You came one day wearing nothing but a tricolour.

OGAREV   What's this, what's this?

NATALIE   It's all nonsense, I was dressed, it was Natalie. (*She laughs freely, then cries out dramatically.*) Where's my little Olga? I promised Natalie!

OGAREV   Olga wasn't born.

It becomes obvious that Ogarev is a physical wreck. He sits at the table.

NATALIE   What difference does that make? Born or unborn, it was her dying wish.

HERZEN   Olga's asleep. Sit down, sit down—when did you eat? There's plenty . . .

OGAREV   Is there a drink?

NATALIE   Well, we'll get her up in a minute.

Malwida, half understanding, speaks to Herzen.

NATALIE (*cont.*)   Then she'll remember all her life how we met.

HERZEN   Malwida says she'll be up all night with the excitement.

NATALIE   'Malwida!' Charming name. Well, don't worry about that—she can have a lie-in while I take the children out.

Natalie takes off her coat and throws it anywhere. Malwida picks it up and places it. Herzen, meanwhile, has been supplying a bottle and a glass to Ogarev, who knocks back a drink and refills his glass.

OGAREV I'm exhausted.

HERZEN How did you come?

OGAREV Berlin—Brussels—Ostend. It wasn't the journey, it was the shopping. She can't pass a toy shop, a hat shop, a shoe shop . . . (*to Tata*) What size are you? Well, never mind, you're the right size for toys and trinkets.

TATA We're not allowed toys.

NATALIE What nonsense is that?

SASHA What did you get me, Natalie?

NATALIE I got you myself, isn't that enough? . . . And . . . ! (*She snatches up a parcel and hands it to Sasha.*)

OGAREV Well, Berlin hasn't changed, except that you can now smoke in the street.

NATALIE (*to Tata*) And, and, and . . . (*to Ogarev*) How are you feeling, Nick?—He's not well.

Sasha opens the parcel, which contains a cheap 'toy' telescope.

SASHA (*to Malwida, forgetting language*) Can I go outside and try it, Malwida?

MALWIDA *Qu'est-ce que vous . . . ?*

Sasha dashes out.

The Parlourmaid hurries in with a loaded tray and sets about reorganising the table.

Natalie gives Tata a parcel and sits down in Malwida's place, investigating the soup tureen. She starts ladling soup around.

HERZEN   Tell me everything! (*to the Parlourmaid*) For the next two days I'm not at home to anyone—do you understand?

TATA (*laughs*)   No, she doesn't, Papa!

HERZEN   'Nobody's to be admitted for the next two days— nobody at all.' (*resuming*) How are all my friends?

OGAREV (*laughs*)   You haven't got any friends. First of all, your scepticism—no, your wholesale slaughter—in your despatches from the revolution—

HERZEN   Completely vindicated!

OGAREV   That makes it worse. Your friends had hardly forgiven you when your pamphlet on so-called revolutionary ideas in Russia arrived . . .

Sasha dashes back in.

SASHA   There's no moon. (*He 'tries out' his telescope in all directions.*)

HERZEN   I only named people who were dead.

OGAREV   Count Orlov boasted, 'It's from the dead we can work our way back to the living if we care to!' Your friends could have wrung your neck. Sasha, you don't know what it was like at home after '48, you can't imagine.

TATA   'Sasha!'

SASHA   Do you call Papa 'Sasha'?

OGAREV   Naturally—he was only as old as you when we became friends.

NATALIE   Is this English soup?

HERZEN (*to Malwida*)   *Asseyez-vous, asseyez-vous.* [Sit down, sit down.]

Malwida takes the sixth chair.

HERZEN (*cont.*)   I'm listening.

OGAREV   You couldn't move, it was dangerous to think, to dream—even to show you weren't afraid—the air we breathed seemed thick with fear. There was a cookbook censored for commending the free circulation of fresh air.

TATA (*opening her parcel*)   Lace!

NATALIE   *Brussels* lace!

Tata jumps up, hoicks up her skirt to accommodate the lace petticoat.

OGAREV   None of us thanked you for granting our adolescent fumblings the status of revolutionary ideas—you elevated a kiss in the corner into free love.

NATALIE   *Pas devant les enfants!* [Not in front of the children.]

MALWIDA (*worried*)   *Excusez moi . . . ?*

TATA   Look at me!

HERZEN (*aware of Malwida*)   Sit down—eat your soup. (*resuming*) Under Tsar Nicholas it was all or nothing—all ideas were revolutionary when thought itself was subversive.

OGAREV   Preaching socialism from London didn't make you friends among your friends at home.

HERZEN (*thrilled*)   You read my pamphlets?

TATA   Thank you, Natalie!

NATALIE   No more presents till you've had your soup.

HERZEN   You were reading the *Free Russian Press*?

OGAREV   What is this soup?

SASHA It's called Brown Windsor. The Queen has it every day.

OGAREV Well, she can have mine.

TATA I don't like it either.

OGAREV Then why are you eating it?

TATA (*enlightened*) Oh, yes! (*pushing her plate aside*) I've finished, Natalie.

SASHA So have I, Natalie.

NATALIE Well, let's see now . . . (*Natalie picks out a small parcel for each of them.*)

MALWIDA (*appealing to Herzen*) Alexander . . . !

HERZEN You were reading the *Free Russian Press*.

OGAREV I told you—Herzen in London was the only candle still alight.

HERZEN I didn't know.

OGAREV But socialism in Russia!—it's utopian, Sasha.

HERZEN So we can expect nothing from Granowski, Ketscher, Botkin, the old gang.

OGAREV There's not much sign of a young gang.

HERZEN Well, I've taken a vow of silence about socialism. We have to move forward looking at our feet, not at the horizon, and we stub our toes on serfdom, censorship, corporal punishment . . . If the Tsar frees the serfs, I'll drink his health—and after that, we'll see.

Sasha and Tata, with a harmonica and a bangle, whoop their thanks and hug Natalie. Ogarev, who has been drinking steadily, suddenly has a mild epileptic fit. Herzen jumps up. Natalie comes expertly to Ogarev's aid.

HERZEN (*cont.*)   What is it?

NATALIE   It's all right—I know what to do.

She does it, and Ogarev calms.

NATALIE (*cont.*)   He's not well. He should see a doctor . . . There.

HERZEN   What happened to you?

NATALIE   He doesn't eat properly. He's all right . . . leave him alone . . . You must stay in bed tomorrow, sweetheart.

OGAREV   No, we're going to see the sights.

SASHA   We've got lessons.

NATALIE   It's educational, seeing the sights.

TATA   Can we go to the waxworks?

SASHA   She means the guillotine with Robespierre's head chopped off. Malwida won't let us.

NATALIE   Oh yes, let's see that.

MALWIDA (*to Natalie*)   *Excusez-moi . . . ?*

NATALIE   *Il n'y aura pas d'études demain.* [No lessons tomorrow.]

Malwida stands up.

NATALIE (*cont.*)   I need to visit, where is it?

The Parlourmaid, having returned to service the table and now leaving again, is intercepted by Natalie, who speaks to her and follows her out. Malwida leaves the room for 'next door'.

HERZEN   Malwida . . .

OGAREV 'Malwida', 'Alexander' . . . is this . . . ?

HERZEN Are you mad?

Sasha blows tunelessly into the mouth organ. Herzen catches up with Malwida 'next door', making a conciliatory gesture.

MALWIDA I'm training the children on pedagogic principles which I have studied.

HERZEN Of course. But Ogarev is my oldest friend . . .

MALWIDA There will be lessons tomorrow at the correct time. I wish to make that clear.

HERZEN Of course. Leave it to me.

They are interrupted by screams from Olga upstairs. Malwida runs to the sound. Sasha and Tata also leave the table hurriedly, following Malwida. Distantly, Olga, Natalie and Malwida contribute loudly to a Russian-German slew of howls, comforts and argument.

The Parlourmaid enters to clear the table. Herzen groans to himself. He picks up the Polar Star *and returns to Ogarev.*

PARLOURMAID (*leaving*) I'd scream, too, if I woke up with the Russians on my bed.

Herzen and Ogarev embrace, and leave towards the sounds of Natalie's voice laughingly consoling Olga, who has calmed down.

JUNE 1856

Indoors.

Malwida, dressed to travel, with a capacious bag, waits for Sasha, Tata and Olga to troop in. Tata's socks are, at second or third glance, odd socks.

49

MALWIDA Come closer, and listen to me, and try to remember this moment. I will never forget you. We're saying goodbye today.

SASHA Are you leaving us?

MALWIDA Yes.

TATA Why?

SASHA I know why. I'm sorry, Miss Malwida.

Malwida kisses Sasha and then kisses Tata and Olga.

TATA Are you leaving right this minute?!

MALWIDA Yes. (*She calls.*) Mrs Blainey!

The NURSE *enters.*

MALWIDA (*cont.*) 'Please conduct the children to Madame Ogarev. Tell Mr Herzen, please . . . well, just tell him I'll send for my trunk.'

NURSE I can't say as I blame you—it's all got topsy-turvy, with nothing you can set your clock by . . .

MALWIDA 'Goodbye.' (*pointing to Tata's socks*) 'Matching socks please, Mrs Blainey.'

NURSE Come along, then.

MALWIDA Be good children.

TATA (*to Malwida*) It's like the splinter, isn't it?

Malwida stops, nods and continues out.

JUNE 1856

In cosy domestic intimacy in the late evening, Herzen and Ogarev occupy the armchairs, with Olga asleep and lightly covered on the couch, and Natalie sitting on the floor by the couch and at Herzen's feet.

NATALIE This is what Natalie prayed for with her dying breath. Your wife was a saint, Alexander. It was because she was a saint that she was defenceless against evil. (*to Ogarev*) Don't give me looks—Alexander understands me. I never trusted that German worm from the moment I saw him . . . acting so helpless and all the time worming himself into her innocent open heart—the wife of the only man who befriended him when he was the laughingstock of Paris—yes, Herwegh's romantic good looks didn't impress the German infantry!

She laughs. Herzen leaves the room.

OGAREV My darling . . . if he comes back, don't forget to mention his mother and son drowned at sea.

NATALIE Oh, aren't we allowed to talk about anything that's changed his life completely since we met?—I don't call that friendship. He wants to talk about it.

OGAREV I remember Kolya that last summer at Sokolovo. He was a happy little thing, he didn't know he was deaf.

Herzen enters with a small framed photo.

OGAREV (*cont.*) Well, I saw the doctor. He said I drink too much. I was impressed. He'd never met me in his life.

Herzen gives the photograph to Natalie and resumes his seat.

HERZEN For you.

NATALIE Oh . . . That's just how I remember her!

HERZEN She *was* a saint. A wonderful wife and companion, a devoted mother, a great spirit. . . .

NATALIE   It's true.

HERZEN   Her devotion to me, her remorse, her courage when she faced the madness that man infected her mind with . . . The blows she suffered in her life! And then losing Kolya!— little Kolya . . . Natalie said over and over, 'He must have been so cold, so frightened, seeing the fishes and the lobsters!'

Natalie flashes a look at Ogarev, Herzen wipes his eyes.

HERZEN (*cont.*)   This won't do, this won't do. It's six years without a real friend by me! Oh, my dear friends. (*to Ogarev*) You've been lost, too. (*to Natalie*) You saved him.

Herzen clasps Natalie's hand. She looks up at him devotedly.

OGAREV   She did. She took on a married man going rapidly downhill. But there!—my wife died and I'm a married man again, going downhill at a comfortable pace.

NATALIE   You were a free man wasting yourself on a wife who'd run off.

HERZEN   Well, enough waste . . . Now it's time for him to get back to work. (*Herzen picks up bundles of letters from his desk.*) Look at this. What are we going to do with it all?

OGAREV   We should have a new paper, not thick and expensive like the *Polar Star,* it should be a cheap rag, easy to smuggle, coming out once or twice a month . . . exposing abuses, naming names . . .

HERZEN (*excited*)   I was waiting for you without knowing it. Herzen and Ogarev! Together we'll dream men's dreams more clearly! What shall we call it?

NATALIE (*gazing raptly at Herzen*)   To dream men's dreams . . . !

OGAREV Something short, like a shout . . . A call to arms.

HERZEN (*noticing Olga*) Look at Olga.

NATALIE They like to be with the grown-ups when they're little. I understand children, even though we can't have any. (*kissing Ogarev*) Well, it's not a secret. I admit it was a blow when Nick told me, but it wasn't without its advantages, when Maria wouldn't divorce him and we thought we could never be married . . .

HERZEN (*laughing*) Your wife is a wonderful woman. May I have your permission to kiss her?

Ogarev waves his hand graciously. Herzen and Natalie kiss chastely. Herzen picks up Olga.

OGAREV It's just like life—waking up in your own bed and not knowing how you got there.

Herzen carries Olga out. Ogarev and Natalie exchange a long look, Ogarev philosophically, Natalie defiantly.

NATALIE What? (*She collapses on Ogarev's lap and starts to weep.*)

JANUARY 1857

Exterior.

Herzen and Blanc, dressed for a funeral, take shelter.

BLANC Was it noticed that I was late? I came in by the wrong gate, and the cemetery is so enormous . . .

HERZEN I don't know. I find these affairs depressing.

BLANC You find funerals depressing. That's all right, you don't have to be a controversialist all the time.

HERZEN   I mean the exiles . . . the dying burying their dead. Failure piled upon loss.

BLANC   Worcell wasn't a failure . . . well, he died before his aims were achieved, but they will be achieved by others, and their success will be his success. He did his duty.

HERZEN   What was that?

BLANC   He sacrificed himself for his cause, as men must.

HERZEN   Why must they?

BLANC   Because it's our human duty—to sacrifice ourselves for the well-being of society.

HERZEN   I don't see how the well-being of society is going to be achieved if everybody is sacrificing themselves and nobody's enjoying themselves. Worcell had been in exile for twenty-six years. He gave up his wife, his children, his estates, his country. Who has gained by it?

BLANC   The future.

HERZEN   Ah, yes, the future.

They shake hands.

BLANC   I hope I see you before the next funeral, especially if it's yours.

Blanc leaves.

Natalie enters.

HERZEN   Natalie . . . how did you . . . ? Isn't Nick with you?

Natalie shakes her head. She comes close to Herzen. They kiss on the mouth.

Pause.

HERZEN (*cont.*)   I'm always at the wrong funeral. Kolya's body was never found. There was a young woman rescued from the sea, my mother's maid. For some reason one of Kolya's gloves was in her pocket. So that's all we got back. A glove.

ACT TWO

The Garden of the Herzen house. It is accessible from the house or 'from the road.'

Herzen, aged forty-seven, is sitting in a comfortable garden chair. A young man, who is Sasha grown up, aged twenty now, is nearby, reclining on the grass with a copy of Herzen's magazine, the Bell. *Tata, 'grown up', aged nearly fifteen, flounces backwards across the garden, calling back to a Nurse who is following in charge of Olga, now nearly nine, and of a pram in which an infant (LIZA) is asleep . . . So we are reminded of Herzen's dream at the beginning of the play.*

NURSE Tata! Tata!

TATA I can if I want!—you're not my nurse!

NURSE We'll see what Madame Ogarev says about that!

HERZEN (*continuing to Sasha*) We're printing five thousand copies!—the *Bell* is being read in the Winter Palace itself . . .

Tata storms off into the house, which is or is not visible, and is immediately heard in an argument with Natalie.

OLGA (*meanwhile*) I don't want any tea!

NURSE And don't you be silly, too.

HERZEN (*to Sasha*) Ogarev and I were the first socialists in Russia, before we knew what socialism was.

Ogarev enters the garden, coming in from a walk. There is something of the down-and-out about his appearance.

OLGA (*starting to cry*)   You can't make me.

HERZEN   We read anything we could get hold of. We took from Rousseau, Saint-Simon, Fourier . . .

Tata storms back from the house.

TATA   I'm going to kill myself!

OGAREV (*to Tata*)   What's this?

HERZEN   From Leroux, from Cabet . . .

TATA   She treats me like a child.

NURSE   Don't be so rude!

TATA   Not you—her!

OGAREV   Tata, Tata . . . Let me wipe your face . . .

TATA   You as well!

NURSE   You'll wake Liza.

HERZEN   Later we took from Proudhon, from Blanc . . .

Tata continues out.

The baby starts crying. Ogarev bends over the pram and makes soothing noises. Natalie comes crossly from the house.

NURSE (*to the pram*)   Look, it's Daddy come to see you.

NATALIE   Beetroot! Did you see?

HERZEN (*to Sasha*)   From Proudhon the abolition of authority . . .

NATALIE (*to the Nurse*)   And what's the matter with her?

NURSE   She says she won't have her tea.

OLGA (*angrily*)   I said I won't eat the fat!

HERZEN (*to Olga*)   Give me a kiss.

NATALIE   I won't give you any fat. Stop crying or I'll give you an enema.

HERZEN   From Rousseau, the nobility of man in his natural state . . .

Ogarev greets Natalie, who embraces him emotionally and bursts into tears.

HERZEN (*cont.*)   (*to Sasha*) From Fourier, the harmonious community, the abolition of competition . . .

The Nurse takes the pram to the house. Natalie breaks the embrace emotionally and follows the Nurse.

NATALIE (*to Olga*)   Come along, you're over-tired, that's what! Early to bed!

OLGA   I'm not tired! I'm not! (*Olga mutinously retreats into the garden, out of sight.*)

HERZEN (*meanwhile*)   From Blanc, the central role of the workers . . .

OGAREV   Stop boring the poor boy, he's going to be a doctor.

HERZEN   From Saint-Simon—

OGAREV (*nostalgically*)   Ah, Saint-Simon. The rehabilitation of the flesh.

SASHA   What's that?

OGAREV   We all get our bodies back, taken from us by Christian guilt. Yes, that was a good one, Saint-Simon's utopia . . . the organisation of society by experts, and as much you-know-what as you want.

HERZEN Pardon me, it was the development of man's whole nature, moral, intellectual, artistic—not just our sensuality . . . in the case of which, some of us didn't need encouragement.

OGAREV Yes, but without the shame, without the confessing and swearing never to do it again.

HERZEN I meant you.

OGAREV I meant me, too.

HERZEN Be a good boy and fetch me a glass of red wine.

OGAREV When it came to love, I was curably romantic. And a glass of vodka.

Sasha glances at Herzen, who shrugs at Ogarev, and leaves.

HERZEN It's not me. It's Natalie. She blames herself for you, and not quietly.

OGAREV Listen, Sasha, don't keep asking Natalie whether she's cross or not. If she puts on a face, ignore it and perhaps things will go better.

HERZEN (*considers*) Yes. Good.

OGAREV (*considers*) On the other hand, ignoring it might set her off. I don't know, it's difficult.

HERZEN Well, you're right. I can't follow her logic.

OGAREV But we must keep her calm, we must help her.

HERZEN You're right. But you, too. When you get drunk, she says we've ruined your life. I don't know what she wants. She wanted you, then she wanted me, then for five minutes she was delirious with joy because we all loved each other, then she decided her love for me was a monstrosity for which she's being punished, and she has dreams where I'm with other women, and I have to deny it, although it was her dream, not mine. She's hysterical. The only thing that calms her down is intimate relations. If only she hadn't got pregnant.

OGAREV   If only you hadn't made her pregnant.

HERZEN   Yes, you're right. Do you want to know how it happened?

OGAREV   Am I to be spared nothing?

HERZEN   It was the night we heard the Tsar had appointed the commission on ending serfdom—and let it be known! —in Russia, where everything happens in secret. It meant we had won. Emancipation was only a matter of agreeing the details. There was no holding back, it had to come, I felt like a conqueror—

OGAREV   Yes, yes, enough, case dismissed. (*Pause.*) And now Liza is nearly a year old.

HERZEN   Ah, yes—well, we knew agreeing on the details would be difficult.

Sasha enters with a glass of red wine, and carefully retrieves from his pocket a glass of vodka. He gives Herzen the wine and Ogarev the vodka. Ogarev knocks back the vodka. Sasha puts the empty glass in his pocket.

OGAREV (*meanwhile*)   The peasants won't wait till Liza's a grandmother. The *Bell* can't wait either.

HERZEN   We've said where we stand—abolition by the pen or by the axe, but by the axe would be a disaster.

OGAREV   I don't find that position entirely clear.

SASHA Natalie was with a visitor.

IVAN TURGENEV *comes from the house, wearing a top hat, with a boutonniere in his frock coat.*

TURGENEV Friends!

HERZEN Turgenev! . . . The wanderer returns.

TURGENEV Oh, I thought I was the Russian on his wanderings, but it's a close thing, you're right. How are you, gentlemen? And young Sasha . . . Is Olga with us? No, she's not. So I can't send her in . . .

HERZEN What's the news? Tell us at once.

TURGENEV First tell me the shotgun I ordered from Lang has found you safely.

HERZEN It's here. We never even took it out of its case.

TURGENEV Well, thank God. I was worried, the way you change houses as if the law was after you.

OGAREV Sasha, perhaps a drink for . . .

TURGENEV No, nothing. (*to Sasha*) I have a message from Natalie. Please find Tata, dead or alive, and nothing more will be said about you-know-what.

SASHA I don't know what. (*Laughs.*) Tata?

TURGENEV I'm only quoting. And Olga, if you see her.

SASHA She's always hiding. Are you going to the opera?

TURGENEV (*put out*) The opera . . . ? Why?

OGAREV He means dressed like that.

TURGENEV Ah . . .

OGAREV How is everything with your opera singer?

TURGENEV Ogarev, that is slightly presumptuous.

OGAREV Well, I'm slightly drunk. (*to Sasha*) He's going to his club.

TURGENEV (*to Sasha*) Dead or alive.

Sasha leaves, calling for Tata.

TURGENEV (*cont.*) (*confidentially*) A little matter of becetroot juice on the cheekbones. (*to Ogarev*) I've got a club. I'm a member of the Athenaeum. I've met Carlyle, Macaulay, Thackeray, Disraeli, I nearly met Lord Palmerston. I think you'll agree, none of your couriers has covered his tracks with half my panache. There's a package of letters I've left indoors, and the latest *Contemporary,* though God knows one doesn't take much pleasure in it. How did a magazine started by Pushkin get into the hands of these literary Jacobins? That's somebody else I've met—D'Antes, the man who killed Pushkin, met him in Paris, you'll never guess where. Dinner at the Russian Embassy! Can you imagine? 'Ere those shoes were old . . .' So that's what our masters think of literature.

OGAREV Did you leave?

TURGENEV Leave? No. I should have done. I never thought of that. Can't we go inside? It's damp.

HERZEN It's damp inside. There's nothing the matter with you.

TURGENEV How would you know? You haven't got my bladder.

OGAREV How long were you in Paris?

TURGENEV Hardly at all, I was . . . in the country, shooting. (*to Ogarev*) Yes, with my friends the Viardots.

OGAREV There's rumours, you know, that she's never let you . . . It's a scandal! (*Ogarev leaves towards the house.*)

TURGENEV What's the matter with him?

HERZEN He needs a drink.

TURGENEV Hardly.

HERZEN What's the news from home?

TURGENEV I'm going to give my new novel to Katkov.

HERZEN To the *Russian Herald*? Everyone will think you've joined the reactionary camp.

TURGENEV I can't help that. You've seen what those thugs Chernyshevsky and Dobrolyubov have done to the *Contemporary*. They despise me. I have my dignity . . . Well, not to mention artistic principles. I was the one who defended Chernyshevsky, you know, when he made his debut with the discovery that you can't eat a painted apple, so art is merely life's poor relation; paintings of the sea are only useful for people living in the middle of Russia who don't know what the sea looks like. I stood up for him. 'Yes,' I said, 'yes, these are the ravings of an infantile bigot, the stinking vomit of a vulture without the first understanding of art—but,' I said, 'there is something here which shouldn't be ignored; the man has made a connection with something vital in the times.' I invited him to dinner. It didn't stop him using my last story as a stick to beat me for being a gentleman and therefore incapable of the positive action needed to save Russia . . . all because the hero of my tale is an indecisive lover! Apparently, that means he's a liberal. Oh, yes, that's the other thing. The word 'liberal' has now entered the scatological vocabulary, like 'halfwit' or 'hypocrite' . . . It means anyone who supports peaceful reform over violent revolution. Our generation of repentant gentry comes off very badly, lumped in with indecisive lovers and slugabeds from Onegin to Oblomov—we're all examples of the same disease, an egotistical upper-class weakness with its roots in the social corruption of a society based on serfdom. (*Pause.*) Well, that makes sense, probably. Dobrolyubov is only twelve years old, you know. Well, he's a child, anyway, he may be twenty-two. I was introduced to him when I looked in at the office. A surly specimen, utterly humourless, a fanatic, he gave me the creeps. I invited him to dinner. Do you know what he said? He said, 'Ivan Sergeyevich, don't let's go on talking to each other. It bores me.' And he walked off to the far corner of the room. I'm their star writer! Well, I was. (*Pause.*) There's something fascinating about them.

HERZEN   'Very dangerous!' It's as if some people only half read the *Bell,* the half that infuriates them. Chernyshevsky denounces us because we urge the Tsar not to let up on the landowners and the bureaucracy. The liberals and the conservatives denounce us because we urge the peasants to keep their axes ready if all else fails. But reform from above or revolution from below, freeing the serfs is an absolute.

TURGENEV   And then what? The *Bell* is as coy as an old maid, but every so often you and Ogarev can't resist lifting your skirts to show what's hiding there—and look!—it's the Russian peasant! He's so different from those Western peasants, so natural and unspoiled, just wait till he comes out from under the skirts and rises to his full height, he'll show those French intellectuals how *Russian* socialism will redeem their bankrupt revolution . . . smothering capitalism in the cradle while the West continues down the road to famine, war, pestilence and useless ornaments in dubious taste. Personally, I only denounce you as sentimental fantasists. You're talking to a man who's made a literary reputation out of the Russian peasantry, and they're no different from Italian, French or German peasants. Conservatives *par excellence*. Give them time and they'll be a match for any Frenchman when it comes to bourgeois aspirations and middle-class mediocrity. We're Europeans, we're just late, that's all. Would you mind if I emptied my bladder into your laurels? (*He moves away.*)

HERZEN Isn't that what you just did? So what if we are cousins in the European family?—It doesn't mean we have to develop in the same way, knowing where it leads to. (*angrily*) I can't have this conversation while you're—

He is interrupted by Turgenev's startled exclamation, followed by a greeting. Turgenev returns discomfited, with Olga.

TURGENEV Hello. Did I startle you? I was just . . . looking at . . .

Tata and Sasha follow unconcernedly. Ogarev and Natalie come from the house.

NATALIE Olga! In! . . .

Olga runs to the house.

TATA (*to Turgenev*) It's our blackbird's nest.

NATALIE Tata, there you are.

TATA Did you see it?

NATALIE I've got something for you, my darling.

TATA (*grudgingly*) What?

NATALIE Well, I wouldn't like to waste it on a face like that . . . Here you are. (*She gives Tata a little pot of rouge.*)

TATA Rouge . . . ? Oh—thank you, Natalie . . . I'm sorry.

Natalie and Tata go into a weeping embrace, thanking, apologising, forgiving, etc.

HERZEN (*to Turgenev*) All finished?

Turgenev shakes his head.

TATA Can I go and try it?

NATALIE Let me.

HERZEN What's all this?

Natalie applies a little rouge to Tata's cheeks.

NATALIE Woman's business. Don't go out wearing it, mind.

HERZEN (*to Sasha*) Will you show Turgenev where . . .

SASHA (*pointing to the laurels*) There.

TURGENEV How grown up everyone is. (*to Sasha*) Natalie tells me you're going to do your studies in Switzerland.

SASHA Yes—medical school. I'll be coming home for vacation.

HERZEN (*to Turgenev*) You'll stay to dinner.

NATALIE He can't, he's going to the opera.

TATA I want to go and look in the mirror. (*Tata leaves to the house.*)

TURGENEV Yes, yes, I am, as a matter of fact.

OGAREV Ah. Good.

Turgenev leaves with Sasha.

Herzen, Natalie and Ogarev settle themselves.

HERZEN (*Pause.*)   So, how are you today? Still cross? No—
just say. Are you cross or not? Oh, I can see you are.

NATALIE   Why, what am I doing?

HERZEN   You're just cross, don't deny it. It's because of what
I said yesterday at the zoo.

NATALIE   What did you say?

HERZEN   Listen, you mustn't take every general remark
personally.

NATALIE   I don't know what you're talking about.

HERZEN   Now, don't get cross.

*Ogarev, irritated beyond patience, abruptly leaves, to the house.
Natalie starts crying.*

HERZEN (*cont.*)   And he's all nerves, too. Please don't cry.

NATALIE   He's in pain. We've broken his heart. His worst
enemy couldn't have hurt him more.

HERZEN   He's gone to get a drink.

NATALIE   And why do you think he drinks?

HERZEN   Oh, come, come, Ogarev used to drink the alcohol
out of the test tubes at university.

NATALIE   You're so *right* all the time. Even when you're in
the wrong, you're so sure you know better than anyone.
Nick, who's truly in the right, is the only one of us who
makes no fuss about this . . . this mistaken dream of a
beautiful life together. You love me, but it's not the deep
pure love we talked about, not the love which transcends

the day-to-day pettiness of normal human failings, which are mostly mine, I know . . .

HERZEN Not at all, only—you mustn't get so . . .

NATALIE I only wish Nicholas could love me with your indifference.

HERZEN Natalie, Natalie—

NATALIE No, I can't do it anymore. I've thought about it. I'm going home to Russia. I've told Nick.

HERZEN What . . . ?

NATALIE He says I shouldn't sacrifice myself—that I should let myself enjoy your love as best I can—but—

HERZEN As best you can? How can you go to Russia—how can you leave the children?

NATALIE I can take Liza.

HERZEN Take our daughter to Russia? For how long?

NATALIE I don't know. I want to see my sister.

HERZEN What about Olga? Who'll look after her?

NATALIE Malwida will.

HERZEN Malwida . . . ? How do you know? My God, am I the last one to be told . . . ?

NATALIE I'm going to Russia! I've done enough harm here. Nick's killing himself because of me!

There is a gunshot. Natalie jumps up and runs towards the house, meeting Ogarev, who has an opened letter. Natalie collapses weeping on his breast.

OGAREV Now, now . . . now, now . . . what's all this? Look what I've got here—a letter from Bakunin!—from Siberia!

HERZEN Bakunin! Is he free?

OGAREV Released into exile. A reader's letter!

HERZEN Praise be! Is he well?

OGAREV Quite his old self, I'd say. It's a letter of complaint about the *Bell*.

NATALIE (*to Ogarev*) I've told Alexander—I'm going home!

Natalie leaves. Herzen takes the letter and starts reading it.

OGAREV Ah, that's another thing. (*Ogarev takes an envelope from his pocket.*) From the Russian Embassy—a formal summons to return . . . I can't obey it, so . . . they won't let Natalie go home now, we'll both be banished. She's going to be dreadfully . . .

Turgenev enters with his new double-barrelled shotgun.

TURGENEV Your son is a joker. I asked him if there were any birds of prey in Fulham, and he very kindly allowed me to shoot his kite.

Sasha enters backwards, tugging on a nearly vertical kite string. Turgenev aims and fires the second barrel.

HERZEN It's some kind of dream.

The blackbird sings in the laurels. Turgenev takes a mock shot at it.

JUNE 1859

There is a small area of gaslight: a street corner in a West End slum. Sounds include drunken argument, laughter, a pianola. Ogarev is with MARY SUTHERLAND.

Mary, aged thirty, is not on the bottom-most rung of society nor of prostitution. She speaks schooled English in a London working-class

accent. Ogarev speaks broken English in a heavy Russian accent. The
dialogue as written does not take account of pronunciation.

OGAREV Mary!

MARY You turned up again. (*friendly*) Do you want to go
with me? (*Ogarev hesitates, searching for words.*) I pleased you,
didn't I? (*Ogarev nods.*) Well, then, what's the long face for?

OGAREV You are right, of course. There was no arrangement.
And, after all, thirty shillings is not a fortune.

MARY God, your accent is something chronic!

OGAREV How is Henry?

MARY Oh, well, so you remember his name.

OGAREV Of course.

MARY Now, listen, I know what you said, but it's easy to say,
it's not money in the bank. It could have been the last I saw
of you.

OGAREV But I was serious.

MARY They're always serious.

OGAREV But I am serious.

MARY Oh, all right, then. If you're serious. Seventeen-and-
six Henry's boarding-out costs me. If I have him with me,
we'll get along nicely on thirty shillings, and you could visit,
there'll be nobody else, I swear.

OGAREV Then all is good. We will meet on Putney Bridge
tomorrow, twelve o' clock, and we find you and Henry a
nice lodging.

MARY Putney! Will there be cows?

OGAREV Perhaps.

MARY All right. Why not?

Ogarev takes Sasha's old harmonica from his coat pocket.

OGAREV For Henry. It's a little broken. (*He plays a little broken tune and offers it to her.*)

MARY You give it to him tomorrow. Do you want to—? It's paid for.

OGAREV With your permission.

MARY Have you got a little boy, too, then?

OGAREV Ah, it is a sad Russian story.

MARY Oh dear, I'm sorry. What happened?

OGAREV It was winter. With my children I make hurry home through the forest in my . . . whoosh . . . !

MARY Your sledge!

OGAREV Precisely. Then I hear the wolves!

MARY No!

OGAREV I see the wolves coming after, coming closer . . . One by one I am forced to throw the children from the sledge . . .

MARY What?!

OGAREV First little Ivan, then Pavel, Fyodor . . . Katerina, Vasilly, Elizaveta, the twins, Anna and Mikhail . . .

They leave arm in arm, Mary laughing.

JULY 1859

The garden. Herzen is alone with NICHOLAS
CHERNYSHEVSKY, *who is thirty-one, red-haired, with a tenor
voice which is sometimes shrill, though presently he is calm and
serious. He is to become, after his death, one of the early saints of the
Bolshevik calendar. He is glancing negligently at a copy of the* Bell.

CHERNYSHEVSKY (*accented*)   'Very Dangerous!' . . . (*continuing
unaccented*) Dobrolyubov and I argued about why the title
was in English.

HERZEN (*shrugs*)   I saw it on a sign somewhere.

CHERNYSHEVSKY   At the zoo, perhaps. Your article made you
many friends, not just among liberals—among the
reactionaries, too.

HERZEN   Of course. They're delighted when there's a
disagreement in our ranks, even if it's only about . . . well,
what was it about, in reality?—a tone of voice, a certain
lack of grace towards your predecessors. Why shouldn't I
defend my generation from the ingratitude of history? They
gave up social position, career, the comfortable
advancement which was their inheritance—because in the
Tsar's autocracy, there was no place for them that could be
filled by sensitive human beings. But the tone of dissent has
altered. It's harsh, jaundiced . . . a monastic order that
excommunicates men for enjoying their dinner, and
pictures and music. The gaiety has gone out of opposition.

CHERNYSHEVSKY   Gaiety.

HERZEN   Yes.

CHERNYSHEVSKY   I wanted to serve humanity, but I was a
physical coward, so I spent part of my youth trying to

invent a perpetual motion machine. In the end, I . . . lost
my momentum. When I got married—this was eight years
ago, when I returned home to Saratov from university—I
told my bride how I thought my life would be.
'Revolution is only a matter of time,' I told her. 'When it
comes, I'll have to take part. It could end in forced labour
or the gallows.' I asked her, 'Are you upset by this talk?
Because I can't talk of anything else. It may go on for
years. And what are the chances for a man who thinks this
way? Here's an example for you,' I said. 'Herzen. I admire
him more than any other Russian. There's nothing I
wouldn't do for him'. (*Pause.*) I read *From the Other Shore*
and *Letters from France and Italy*. It wasn't your gaiety, it
was your grief, your fury . . . but yes, the stylishness, too,
oh the flash and slash of your scorn, your logic, how you
dealt with pomposity, delusion, pettiness . . . ! I marvelled
at you. And now I find I can't read you anymore. I don't
want brilliance. It turns my stomach. I want the black
bread of facts and figures, analysis, projection. It's hard
graft. I'm crushed by work. You and your friends lived the
usual life of the upper classes. Your generation were the
romantics of the cause, the dilettanti of revolutionary
ideas. You *liked* being revolutionaries, if that's what you
were. Well, that's better than wanting to be senators and
generals. But with people like me, it wasn't a case of
sacrificing our social position, it was *because* of our social
position. Every day was a fight for life—against crop
failure, cholera, horse thieves, brigands, huge packs of
wolves . . . The only escape from the misery was to be a
drunkard or a holy fool, of which we had many. I don't
like my life. And there are things now I won't do for you.

HERZEN Such as what?

CHERNYSHEVSKY   I won't believe in the good intentions of the Tsar. I won't believe in the good intentions of the government: authority will not undermine itself. Above all, I won't listen to babbling about progress. While the commission argues about terms, the serfs are being exploited more than ever as the nobility fights to keep its privileges. The case for reform is delusion. Only the axe will do.

HERZEN   And then what?

CHERNYSHEVSKY   We will have to see. First the social revolution, then the political. Organisation on a full belly.

HERZEN   It's not the belly, it's the head. Organisation? The wolf packs will have the freedom of the streets of Saratov! Who will do the organising? Oh, but of course!—you will! The revolutionary elite. Because the peasants aren't to be trusted, they're too ignorant, too feckless, too drunk. Which they are. And what if they don't want you? If they'd rather eat or be eaten like everyone else? Will you coerce them for their own good? Will you be their Little Father? You'll need some help. You might have to have your own police force. Chernyshevsky!—are we ridding the people of their yoke so that they can live under a dictatorship of the intellectuals? Only until the enemy has been liquidated, of course!—that's Proudhon's word, and a good one. In Paris I saw enough wet blood in the gutters to last me. Progress by peaceful steps. I'll babble it as long as I've got breath.

CHERNYSHEVSKY   Good. That's clear. I told Dobrolyubov, the only thing was for me to come and talk to you face-to-face, and then we'll know why the *Bell*—our hallowed *Bell,* the only free voice in the Russian tongue, which has called to us to come forward and find each other—*that Bell*—refuses to agitate for a revolution.

HERZEN   That would suit the government very well—it would drive the reformists into the arms of the conservatives.

CHERNYSHEVSKY   Oh yes, 'very dangerous.' Your article practically accuses me of being in the pay of the government. Dobrolyubov wanted to challenge you to a duel—as our chief critic, he is over-exposed to literature.

HERZEN   The *Bell* needs a typeface for irony. Do you want a retraction?

CHERNYSHEVSKY   There's no need. It's clear enough that the government should be paying you. Your muckraking isn't progress, it's the opposite. The more the system mends its ways, the longer it will survive.

HERZEN   So let corruption thrive—but at whose cost meanwhile?

Ogarev enters.

CHERNYSHEVSKY   It's piecemeal. What is your *programme*?

OGAREV   The abolition of serfdom from above or below, except from below. Obviously I've missed nothing important. You're Chernyshevsky . . . Ogarev. In England we make 'le shake-hand.'

CHERNYSHEVSKY   (*shaking hands*)   I'm glad to meet you.

OGAREV   I, too. Forgive me . . . (*glancing at Herzen*) Visiting a sick friend. Have you been waiting ages?

CHERNYSHEVSKY   No, not at all. I got lost.

OGAREV   Did you ask a policeman?

CHERNYSHEVSKY   A policeman? No.

OGAREV You should. They call you 'sir' and seem to be a kind of public service. They're for people who are lost. They're issued with maps and gazetteers. Often you see them two together so they can consult about the shortest route. You can hardly turn a corner without seeing another one. At night they carry lanterns so they can read the map. A Russian comes here, and naturally all these policemen make him nervous. It's weeks before he can grasp that they're to tell people the way to everywhere. I was just in Putney and I had to ask a policeman the way to the nearest chemist's. (*to Herzen*) Mary's sick. I had to bring her.

HERZEN Bring her . . . ?

OGAREV I couldn't leave her with only Henry. (*to Chernyshevsky*) How long will you stay?

CHERNYSHEVSKY In England? I'm leaving tomorrow.

OGAREV But you've only just arrived. London is worth a study. Every night a hundred thousand people have nowhere to sleep except in the streets, and every morning a certain number of them are dead. They die of starvation beside hotels where you can't dine for less than two pounds. The policemen I was telling you about arrange for the bodies to be taken away. That's their other function. But, at the same time, if you're not dead, a policeman can't take you away. If you have a place to live in, even a hovel, he can't enter at his whim. If he believes you're a criminal, he can lock you up, but he has to show cause to a magistrate in public within a couple of days, or he has to let you go—to starve to death perhaps. With all this liberty, there's no beggar in France or Russia as destitute as the London poor, and with all this poverty, no

Frenchman or Russian has his liberty guarded like a London beggar. It's not just liberty in the policeman sense. You never saw so many eccentrics, human nature tolerated in all its variety. What exactly is going on here? Do poverty and liberty go together, or is it the English sense of humour? We're not looking at what's around us. The political exiles didn't come to England to continue the quest, they retreated here until the quest can be resumed. So we gather here—in this garden or around the table inside—endlessly debating the Russian question of the hour: emancipation with or without land?—with or without compensation?—how much—who pays? over how long?—in rent or in labour? . . . but not what is the best society for everyone everywhere?

HERZEN There's no such thing as 'everyone everywhere.' For Russia—now—the answer is communal socialism.

CHERNYSHEVSKY *Communal* socialism, each household with its own plot, is inefficient. But *communistic* socialism, with everybody sharing the labour and the harvest—

HERZEN (*angrily*) No!—No!—we haven't come all this way only to arrive at the utopia of the ant heap.

Natalie enters pushing Liza's pram.

NATALIE What are you cross about?

She pushes the pram nearer and takes a chair. Chernyshevsky stands up politely for her.

OGAREV (*to Natalie*) Have you . . . ? It's only until . . .

NATALIE (*suddenly*) Alexander! We have, you have a guest!

HERZEN What? It's Chernyshevsky! You gave him a glass of water.

NATALIE (*laughs*) He thinks I'm an idiot. Have you had nothing but a glass of water? I'm ashamed.

CHERNYSHEVSKY It was all I wanted, really.

NATALIE (*to Herzen*) I mean Mrs Sutherland.

HERZEN Who? . . . Oh . . .

NATALIE (*to Chernyshevsky*) One of the Putney Sutherlands.

CHERNYSHEVSKY Oh, yes?

OGAREV (*to Natalie*) You don't mind, do you?

NATALIE It's Alexander's house, not ours, my dear. (*to Herzen*) Oughtn't you to go in and . . . Nick's put her in, in the yellow room.

HERZEN What yellow room?

NATALIE Alexander, there is only one yellow room.

HERZEN The scullery?

NATALIE The room with the yellow roses on the wallpaper.

HERZEN Oh . . . Is she *staying*?

NATALIE That's what we all want to know.

HERZEN (*to Ogarev*) She's not staying?

Ogarev doesn't reply. Liza starts grizzling.

CHERNYSHEVSKY I must be going soon. (*He is ignored. He is uneasily aware of missing something.*)

OGAREV It's only until she's . . .

Liza grizzles louder. Ogarev, grateful for the distraction, goes to the pram and jogs it agitatedly.

NATALIE Nurse is busy helping the maid carry the couch in from the landing.

HERZEN What for?

OGAREV It's for Henry.

HERZEN She's brought her son?

OGAREV Well, what do you expect!

Ogarev thumps the pram. Liza starts crying. Ogarev jogs the pram, talking to Liza.

NATALIE (*to Herzen, forgetting herself*) She wants her daddy.

Herzen is furious. Chernyshevsky is puzzled.

NATALIE (*to Liza, retracting*) There, there, look, Daddy's here . . .

CHERNYSHEVSKY (*to Ogarev, peering at Liza*) She's just like you.

Tata comes from the house.

NATALIE (*to Herzen*) If you don't go, it'll be too late. The maid has already made a scene, and in front of Tata, too.

TATA (*arriving*) What's a 'fancy woman' in England?

NATALIE What a thing to ask, Tata!

TATA (*to Ogarev*) Well, she's in your bed, anyway. She's got a little boy who won't say his name. He's not going to live here, is he? (*to Chernyshevsky*) Oh . . . I'm Tata Herzen!

CHERNYSHEVSKY (*shaking her hand*) Goodbye.

TATA Oh. Goodbye.

Chernyshevsky shakes Ogarev's hand and then bows over Natalie's hand.

TATA *(cont.)* *(to Herzen meanwhile)* Natalie says when she goes to Germany to meet her sister, she'll take me.

HERZEN What about Olga?

TATA You know what they're like together. Anyway, she'll forget her Russian.

HERZEN Why? You'll all be speaking Russian, won't you? Natalie's sister and her husband . . . ?

TATA Oh, Papa!—what's the point of going to Germany to improve my Russian?

CHERNYSHEVSKY *(to Herzen)* Goodbye.

HERZEN You're going?

Herzen shepherds Chernyshevsky a few paces.

NATALIE *(hisses to Ogarev)* Are you mad? She's a . . . she's a . . .

TATA A fancy woman.

NATALIE *(to Tata)* Go in!

Tata leaves.

HERZEN *(to Chernyshevsky)* The thing I feared most was that a gulf would divide the intellectuals from the masses, like in the West. But I never foresaw the worst, that the ground would split between so few of us who want the same thing for Russia.

CHERNYSHEVSKY It's not so wide that you can't make the step.

Natalie, who has been whispering fiercely to Ogarev, walks by, to the house.

HERZEN But I'm right. Even where I'm wrong, I'm right.

NATALIE (*continuing out*) You see?!

CHERNYSHEVSKY Suppose the people don't wait for you.

HERZEN Then you'll see I was right.

CHERNYSHEVSKY They won't wait.

HERZEN They will.

CHERNYSHEVSKY The Tsar will let you down.

HERZEN He won't.

CHERNYSHEVSKY You've bet the *Bell* on it, you'll lose everything.

HERZEN The *Bell* will win.

Herzen and Chernyshevsky leave, following Natalie. Ogarev, in private physical distress, collapses in an epileptic fit. HENRY SUTHERLAND comes into the garden. He is small and underfed, in poor clothes but neat, and afraid. After a moment he notices Ogarev. He goes to help him, evidently not for the first time. Ogarev recovers, collapsed on a chair, mute for the moment. He smiles to reassure Henry, and makes a sign which Henry understands. The boy takes the mouth organ from his pocket and plays haltingly for Ogarev.

INTER-SCENE—AUGUST 1860

Blackgang Chine, a ravine in the southern coastline of the Isle of Wight, notorious for shipwreck.

In a 'soundscape' of waves crashing against rocks, with seabirds shrill in the blasts of wind noise . . . a windswept figure (Turgenev) stands dramatised by the surrounding dark.

AUGUST 1860

Seaside (Ventnor, Isle of Wight).

There is a passing scene of visitors, who greet each other, exchange remarks and move on. Remarkably, all the exchanges are in Russian ('Good morning—How are you this morning?—Charming weather—When are you leaving', and such like) . . . 'Dóbroye óotra—Kak vy pazhíváyetye sevódnya óotram?—Prekrásnaya pagóda / Atlíchnaya pagóda—Kagdá ooyezháyetye? / Kadgá atpravlyáyetes?'

A young man—the DOCTOR—who is noticeably more plainly dressed, is sitting on a bench at the boundary between the promenade and the beach. He has a newspaper, the local weekly. Turgenev enters, and after raising his hat and exchanging greetings with one or two people, he sits on the bench, or a nearby bench. He takes a book from his pocket and reads for a while, then dozes. Meanwhile Malwida and Olga have appeared on the beach. Olga has a shrimping net. Malwida has been collecting shells, putting them into a child's pail.

OLGA Do you think shrimps are happy?

MALWIDA Perfectly happy.

OLGA Do you wish you were a shrimp?

MALWIDA Not very much. No Beethoven, no Schiller or Heine . . .

OLGA You wouldn't mind, if you were a shrimp.

MALWIDA But if I were a shrimp, a little girl might come and catch me in her net.

OLGA That's no worse than what happens to people.

MALWIDA Ah, a philosopher. (*She picks up a shell.*) There's a pretty one . . . a double. Anyone at home? Well, bad luck, you will decorate a picture frame and think yourself lucky compared to some.

OLGA   Is everyone going to get a picture frame for Christmas?

MALWIDA   Oh, aren't we a clever-boots?

OLGA   I'd like a picture frame, Malwida.

MALWIDA   Special people might get a shell mirror.

OLGA   I don't want to see my face, I want to see yours! (*She laughs and hugs Malwida.*) There's a man there who knows Papa.

MALWIDA   We don't look. The one with the newspaper or the other one?

OLGA   The other one. He's called Mr Turgenev. He's a famous writer.

MALWIDA   All Russian writers are famous. In Germany you have to work really hard to be a famous writer.

OLGA   Should we speak to him?

MALWIDA   He looks asleep. I wonder where he's staying.

OLGA   When Papa comes from London, we can invite him. Malwida, what will happen when Natalie comes back from Germany?

MALWIDA   She's only just gone and you're worrying about when she comes back. Come on, there's a rock pool.

OLGA   I want to go on living in your house, and Papa can visit us . . .

MALWIDA   You must try to like Natalie.

OLGA (*thoughtfully*)   I like her sometimes, when she's not historical. When she gets historical, the only thing that calms her down is intimate relations.

Olga and Malwida leave.

Turgenev notices that the Doctor has put aside his newspaper.

TURGENEV   Sir . . . would you please allow me to look at your newspaper?

DOCTOR   Keep it. I've finished with it. (*The Doctor's tone is unsettlingly abrupt.*)

TURGENEV   Thank you. I threw my copy away and forgot that there was something I meant to . . . Ah, here we are . . . Are you sure you don't need it? Because . . . (*Turgenev takes a small penknife from his pocket and cuts carefully into the newspaper.*)

DOCTOR (*meanwhile*)   Are you Turgenev?

TURGENEV   I am.

DOCTOR   Your name—approximately—is in the paper, in the list of notable visitors. How did you know I was Russian?

TURGENEV   It was a statistical probability. One of the mysteries of summer migration in the animal kingdom is that in August a small town in the Isle of Wight becomes a Russian colony . . . But I knew you when I saw you. We've met before, haven't we?

DOCTOR   No.

TURGENEV   In St Petersburg . . . ?

DOCTOR   I doubt it. I'm not one of your literary . . . I'm not one of your readers. I only read books of practical utility.

TURGENEV   Really? I find there are occasions when even such a useful publication as the *Ventnor Times* . . . when you're by the sea, enjoying nature . . .

DOCTOR   Nature? Nature is nothing but the sum of its facts. What you're enjoying is your romantic egoism. (*He has a look at the title of Turgenev's book.*) Pushkin! Not a damn bit of use to anyone! Give it up. You're past the age for this nonsense. A good plumber is worth twenty poets.

TURGENEV   Oh. Are you a plumber?

DOCTOR   No.

TURGENEV   Well, in the sense that there are twenty poets for every good plumber, who would disagree with you? But I like to think my books have their uses beyond stopping up a bunghole.

DOCTOR   Well, they don't. For a *useful* book, give me Mackenzie's *No More Haemorrhoids!*

TURGENEV (*enthusiastically*)   Yes, it's extremely good. (*He holds up the newspaper cutting.*) In case you missed it, there's an advertisement in the paper for Holloway's Pills. Remarkable! (*reading*) '. . . expressly combined to operate on the stomach, the liver, the kidneys, the lungs, the skin and the bowels, purifying the blood, which is the very foundation of life, *and thus curing disease in all its forms* . . .' I thought they sounded worth trying. But to get back to your haemorrhoids—

DOCTOR   I don't suffer from haemorrhoids.

TURGENEV   Oh. I wish I didn't. But in case you ever do, here's a tip. I found that reading Dr Mackenzie made me very aware of mine . . . whereas, reading Pushkin, I quite forgot them. Practical utility. I believe in it.

DOCTOR But what the age demands is to believe in nothing else.

TURGENEV Nothing at all?

DOCTOR Nothing.

TURGENEV You don't believe in principles? Or progress? Or art?

DOCTOR No. I deny abstractions.

TURGENEV But you believe in science.

DOCTOR Abstract science, no. Tell me a fact and I'll agree with you. Two and two is four. The rest is horse shit. You don't need it to know to put bread in your mouth when you're hungry. Believing in nothing, to be precise, means to take nothing on trust, no matter how clothed in authority or tradition . . . Negation is the thing that's best for Russia now.

TURGENEV You mean the people, the masses?

DOCTOR The people!—worse than useless. No, I don't believe in the people. The pedants of the thick magazines and the secret presses bang on about the people, and the role of the intellectual, and the role of the artist, and the role of science, and everything comes to nothing for want of honest men.

TURGENEV What, then, do you advocate?

DOCTOR Nothing.

TURGENEV Literally nothing?

DOCTOR Oh, there are more of us nihilists than you think. We're a force.

TURGENEV Oh, yes . . . the nihilist. You're right, we haven't met before. It's only that I've been looking out for you without knowing it. The other day, the day we had the storm, I went to look at Blackgang Chine. Have you been? It's not far from here, westward along the upper cliff. At the top there's a grassy bit which runs almost to the edge of the drop, four hundred feet straight down to where the sea smashes over the ledges and the pebble shore, hurling itself into the gullet of the ravine they call Blackgang. There's a way down, a snaking path that takes you back across millennia of bands of colour in the rock face, past limestone and black ironstone piled on yellow sandstone, dark-blue clay . . . The noise is indescribable. I thought I could hear groans, sobbing, cannon fire, bells, sounding out from the heart of the furious waters. It was like being at the beginning of the world, where the elemental mocked at our flimsy comforts and only horror and death were promised. I saw there was no hope for us. And there was a man in my mind suddenly, a dark towering figure, strong, with no subtlety or mutability in him, with no history, as though he'd grown from the earth, his ill intention complete. I thought—I've never read about him. Why has nobody written about him? I knew he was the future arrived before his time, and that he was doomed. (*Pause.*) I don't know what to call you.

The accompanying faint reprise of the noise at Blackgang Chine grows. Turgenev and the Doctor stay looking out to sea.

MARCH 1861

Garden. Tata is drawing. Offstage, Liza, aged two, starts bawling. Tata looks round and sighs impatiently. The Nurse enters hurriedly.

TATA   She's in the nettles.

NURSE   You were supposed to be watching.

TATA   I was.

The Nurse goes to rescue Liza. Ogarev enters excitedly with newspapers. Tata is pleased to see him.

TATA (*cont.*) (*to Ogarev*)   Papa went to send you a telegram.

OGAREV   It was even in our little newspaper, can you imagine!

TATA   Is it nice living in Putney?

Ernest Jones, the English Chartist, enters from the house.

JONES   I say!—I say!—Ogarev!—Emancipation!

Jones offers his hand. Ogarev shakes it, then embraces him.

JONES (*cont.*)   Oh, I say!

Blanc, with a bottle of champagne, comes from the house.

BLANC   Ogarev! Felicitations! Where's Herzen?

JONES (*to Tata*)   How proud you must be. The Tsar has justified all the hopes your father had in him.

Herzen hurries in from the side. Natalie, with a bouquet, comes from the house. Blanc presents the bottle to Herzen.

HERZEN   We'll give a party for every Russian in London.

NATALIE   Look what came—from Mazzini!

Herzen and Ogarev embrace. The other men applaud them. Herzen runs to Natalie and swings her off her feet.

HERZEN   We won!

Herzen pops the champagne cork. Everyone piles back into the house, followed now by the Nurse, who is carrying Liza, as it were, and rubbing her face with a handful of dockleaves.

Then it's night with a moon.

DECEMBER 1861

Indoors, with indications of Christmas. Herzen is pacing, with a month-old infant crying lustily in his arms, while Natalie breast-feeds its twin. Ogarev is at a table with paperwork. Natalie's chair or couch is draped in a large red banner used as a throw. Herzen manages to pacify the crying baby somewhat.

HERZEN   We got carried away. Or I did.

NATALIE   Everybody did. It wasn't your fault. The Emancipation was managed in a Russian way. Nothing is explained. Freedom was thrown to the serfs like a bone to a pack of dogs coming after you . . . and written in legal gobbledegook even the village readers couldn't make out, so what can you expect? The peasants are told they're free, and they think the land they've worked now belongs to them, even the big house belongs to them, and the livestock and probably Madame's Paris frocks, too—so when it turns out nothing belongs to them and they have to pay rent for their plots, well, obviously freedom bears an uncanny resemblance to serfdom.

HERZEN   Chernyshevsky must be laughing into his whiskers. Riots on over a thousand estates . . . hundreds killed . . .

The baby starts crying.

HERZEN (*cont.*)   The celebration baked meats did furnish forth the funeral tables. How many guests did we invite?

NATALIE Hundreds.

HERZEN And an orchestra, and seven thousand gas jets to light up the house . . .

NATALIE And my poor banner, look . . .

HERZEN (*exasperated, to Ogarev*) You take him, her, I can't . . .

OGAREV (*taking the baby*) Circulation's down. There's less material coming in, too. We can't sell the paper if we can't fill it . . .

There is a disturbance outside in the hall, a loud voice calling for Herzen.

HERZEN It's Bakunin!

Bakunin bursts in—a huge and hirsute force, an emperor tramp—followed by the Parlourmaid.

HERZEN (*cont.*) You got here!

BAKUNIN What's this? It's time to get to work!

Natalie squeals in modest confusion.

BAKUNIN (*cont.*) Madame! Michael Bakunin! (*He grabs her hand to kiss it, stooping over her.*) There is no more lovely sight than a baby at the breast. (*He grabs Ogarev's hand and shakes it.*) Ogarev. Congratulations! Boys or girls?

OGAREV Who knows?

NATALIE One of each.

OGAREV It's truly amazing to see you. Your escape has made you famous.

HERZEN You're fat!

OGAREV Tell us everything! How did you . . . ?

NATALIE Wait, wait, don't start without me! (*She hands her baby to the Parlourmaid and takes the baby from Ogarev.*)

BAKUNIN Nothing to it—American ship—Japan—San Francisco—Panama—New York. Thanks for sending the money—landed at Liverpool this morning. Can you get oysters here?

HERZEN Oysters? Of course. Send out for four dozen oysters.

Natalie and the Parlourmaid leave with the babies.

BAKUNIN Why, aren't you having any? By the way, can you lend me the money to pay the cab? I'm down to my last . . .

HERZEN (*laughs*) Come on. I'll see to it.

BAKUNIN All for one and one for all. We're going to do great things together with the *Bell*.

Herzen and Ogarev exchange glances.

BAKUNIN (*cont.*) Where's the next revolution? What about the Slavs?

HERZEN All quiet.

BAKUNIN Italy, then?

HERZEN Quiet.

BAKUNIN Germany? Turkey?

HERZEN Everywhere's quiet.

BAKUNIN Good Christ, it's lucky I'm back . . .

Herzen and Bakunin leave. Ogarev remains. He notices the red banner on the couch, and spreads it out. The word 'Freedom' in Russian is embroidered on it. Ogarev shakes out the banner like a blanket.

JUNE 1862

*Simultaneously there is a hubbub. The area round the table is
crowded. Bakunin is at the centre of the activity.*

*From Herzen's memoirs: 'Heaps of tobacco lay on his table like stores
of forage, cigar ash covered his papers, together with half-finished glasses
of tea . . . Clouds of smoke hung about the room from a regular suite of
smokers who smoked as if they were in a smoking race, hurriedly
blowing it out and drawing it in as only Russians and Slavs do smoke.
Many a time I enjoyed the amazement, accompanied by a certain horror
and perplexity, of the landlady's servant when at dead of night she
brought boiling water and a fifth basin of sugar into this hotbed of Slav
emancipation . . . He argued, lectured, made arrangements, shouted,
decided, directed, organised and encouraged all day and all night long
. . . In the brief minutes he had free, he rushed to his writing-table,
cleared a little space from cigarette ash, and set to work to write five, ten,
fifteen letters to Belgrade and Constantinople, to Bessarabia, Moldavia
and White Russia. In the middle of a letter he would fling aside the pen
and bring up to date the outmoded opinion of some Dalmatian, snatch
up his pen and go on writing in an everlasting sweat . . .' This version
of shadowy gesticulating smokers, around the pool of Bakunin's light,
has a barely comprehensible sound track. Bakunin's words are
italicised.*

VOICES *(overlapped)   . . . You can deliver this one to Buda, it's
hardly out of your way. When you get to Zagreb, Romic will be at
the hotel under the name of Jellinek . . .* We have ten thousand
patriots waiting for the signal.—I knew him in Paris. He's
not to be trusted.—They need fifty pounds immediately.—
Half the garrison is with us.—No, the committee must keep
their identity a secret from each other until the time is
ripe.—*Thank you, you're an angel, and another bowl of sugar!*—
And what then? No, you're wrong. Moldavia is quiet apart
from one man I can trust.—*And this to the caucasus. Establish*

*a network and report back to me in the code we agreed—wait, I want to add something.—*Can we trust him?—Trust me. I'm not behaving like a dictator. Who else can be trusted? Yes, I trust you, but you have to trust me.—The question of boundaries can be settled later. The national question can wait, the social question is the basis of the coming revolution. Yes, I hate the Hungarians, too, but Austria is the enemy. The Czechs agree with us.—My article, did you read it?—Five thousand copies distributed in secret.—*That's nonsense! First revolution, then federation. Quiet—quiet!—what's that noise?*

As things quieten, a baby is heard screaming.

BAKUNIN   It's all right, it's only the twins. What time is it? Sssh!

The scene reconstitutes itself as a social gathering in which the Slav conspirators continue much as before, with Herzen at the table adding a few lines to a letter, while a guest, PAVEL VETOSHNIKOV, *stands by to receive it. Bakunin is now concentrating on a Russian officer,* KORF, *whom he leads to Herzen. Korf is young, shy, speechless, in mufti. Natalie brings a glass of cloudy medicine to Turgenev, who is in conversation with a young man,* SEMLOV. *Tata plucks at Natalie for attention. At the same time, Ogarev, replacing the banner over the couch, sees that he is being observed by a guest,* PEROTKIN, *who has a glass of wine and a cigar.*

PEROTKIN   What is that? A banner?

OGAREV   Yes.

PEROTKIN   What does it say?

OGAREV   'Freedom.' My wife made it.

PEROTKIN Sounds a bit desperate. (*Laughing, he introduces himself.*) Perotkin.

Ogarev acknowledges Perotkin but excuses himself and finds a place where he can write. He continues to write, in a notebook. He writes, first, the pages which end up in an envelope in Vetoshnikov's pocket—Herzen having added his postscript; and, also, the page from which he is to read aloud to the company later.

TURGENEV (*to Semlov*) It's quite simple, I called him Bazarov because Bazarov was his name.

NATALIE (*arriving*) There you are . . . (*She gives Turgenev the medicine.*)

TATA (*to Natalie*) Did you ask Papa?

BAKUNIN (*to Herzen*) Lieutenant Korf has to leave for Wallachia, it's desperately urgent.

HERZEN (*writing*) One moment.

TURGENEV (*swallowing the medicine*) Ugh . . . thank you.

TATA (*to Natalie*) If he won't, I'll kill myself.

SEMLOV (*examining the pillbox*) Hang on, it's a suppository . . .

NATALIE (*to Tata*) I can't ask him now—go up. I'll come and see you.

Tata leaves.

HERZEN (*to Bakunin*) Twenty pounds for the Lieutenant?

BAKUNIN For the cause. He's a splendid fellow. It would be a sin to let the chance slip.

Perotkin joins Turgenev as Semlov departs laughing.

SEMLOV (*to a guest*) Did you hear? Turgenev . . .

HERZEN (*to Bakunin*)   No, leave him be.

TURGENEV   Who was that fool?

PEROTKIN   He's a friend of Bakunin. I trust him completely
. . . Perotkin—I'm a friend of Bakunin. I read your book. I
wish I could say . . .

TURGENEV   You don't have to.

HERZEN (*to Korf, shaking hands*)   Come to lunch on Sunday.
Enjoy yourself—go to the International Exhibition . . .

*Herzen seals the letter and gives it to Vetoshnikov. Bakunin leads
Korf away, reassuring him.*

BAKUNIN   Leave it to me.

TURGENEV (*to Perotkin*)   Some people liked it . . . elderly
generals who thanked me for exposing the criminal
boneheadedness of the nihilists . . . and one or two young
critics who expressed their gratitude for my sympathy with
Bazarov's fearless honesty and intelligence . . . but in general
I'm being called a traitor by both the left and the right, on
the one hand for my malicious travesty of radical youth, and
on the other hand for sucking up to it.

PEROTKIN   And what was your attitude really?

TURGENEV   My attitude?

PEROTKIN   Yes, your purpose?

TURGENEV   My purpose? My purpose was to write a novel.

PEROTKIN   So you don't take sides between the fathers and
the children?

TURGENEV   On the contrary, I take every possible side.

Bakunin draws Turgenev aside.

TURGENEV (*cont.*)   Who is that fool?

BAKUNIN   I don't know.

TURGENEV   But you brought him, he's a friend of yours.

BAKUNIN   Oh, yes. He's one of us. Listen, this is the last thing I'll ever ask of you . . .

TURGENEV   Before you go on, I've already given you fifteen hundred francs. You could make twenty or thirty thousand francs by writing the story of your escape . . .

BAKUNIN   It's beneath me to write for money.

Perotkin joins a group who by now have interrupted Herzen several times to shake his hand. Among them is SLEPTSOV, a young man.

SLEPTSOV (*to Herzen*)   I can't believe I'm talking to you. It was the *Bell* which called us into existence—thousands of us! . . . and gave us our name. 'The people want two things,' you wrote, 'land and liberty!'

HERZEN (*shaking hands*)   That was Ogarev . . . Thank you . . .

SLEPTSOV   Let them know the *Bell* is with us!

Sleptsov leaves. Vetoshnikov is almost the last of the visitors to leave. Herzen shakes his hand.

SLEPTSOV (*cont.*)   Thank you, Vetoshnikov. Have you got everything safe?

VETOSHNIKOV   Yes.

PEROTKIN (*arriving, to Vetoshnikov*)   Vetoshnikov, should we look for a cab together?

VETOSHNIKOV   No, I want to walk.

PEROTKIN Of course. Good night. (*to Herzen*) Thank you again. Where would we all be without your hospitality?

HERZEN Come to lunch on Sunday. It's open house.

PEROTKIN I will. (*Perotkin leaves with the stragglers.*)

OGAREV (*to Vetoshnikov*) If you can make a few copies, Vetoshnikov, when you get to St Petersburg . . .

VETOSHNIKOV (*patting his pocket*) Don't worry.

HERZEN (*to Ogarev*) I added a few lines for Chernyshevsky, to tell him if the *Contemporary* is shut down, we'll print it in London.

Vetoshnikov leaves. There is now only a residual group of intimates—Herzen, Natalie, Ogarev, Bakunin and Turgenev. Ogarev tears a page from his notebook and joins the others.

NATALIE (*to Turgenev*) I put a warming pan in your bed.

OGAREV How long are you here for this time?

TURGENEV A week. I'm buying a dog.

NATALIE A bulldog?

TURGENEV No, a gundog.

OGAREV Won't it have to know Russian?

BAKUNIN (*to Ogarev*) Read it out.

Ogarev reads from his notebook.

OGAREV 'Land and Liberty! The words have a familiar sound. Land and Liberty was the theme of our every article. Land and Liberty was blazoned on every sheet that was issued by our London Press. We greet you, brothers, on the common path . . .'

BAKUNIN   Good! We should take over the direction of the whole network in Russia!

HERZEN   Oh, it's we. So you've realised your Slavs couldn't row a boat together, never mind overthrow the Austrian Empire, and now Land and Liberty is your new enthusiasm until you meet someone who tells you the man in the moon has a network, too, and a better one. The *Bell* has moved Russia—helped to—forward painfully for six years, and these *children* invite us to be their London office!

BAKUNIN   I'm truly disgusted with you. We can't sit forever with our arms folded while these thousands of brave young men—

HERZEN   You really are a big Liza! (*to Ogarev*) You didn't believe that, did you?

OGAREV (*uncomfortably*)   It's a question of giving a helping hand. If they were strong, they wouldn't need us.

HERZEN   No, it's a question of what they believe in, and what we *don't* believe in—a secret revolutionary elite.

TURGENEV   Quite right.

HERZEN   What's it got to do with you?

TURGENEV   I'm agreeing with you.

HERZEN   You agree with everyone a little.

TURGENEV   Well, up to a point.

HERZEN (*to Ogarev*)   We'd be putting our names to exactly what we told Chernyshevsky we wouldn't support— agitation for violent revolution.

OGAREV We're all on the side of the people, aren't we?

HERZEN They look on the people as lumps of clay and themselves as the sculptors. We have more to learn than to teach. The people will make their own Russia. But we have to be patient. Why should we have to put the *Bell's* reputation on a fledgling which will die in the nest?

OGAREV Because we do. I don't care if Land and Liberty is only twelve people. They occupy the only ground not occupied by the government and its supporters.

BAKUNIN Well, it's two against one.

HERZEN (*snaps*) You haven't got a vote, and I haven't used mine.

NATALIE (*to Herzen*) Nick's right. You're not wrong, but Nick's right.

TURGENEV You see? . . . At home we had an English clock with a little brass lever that said, (*accented*) 'Strike—Silent' . . . It was the first English I knew . . . 'Strike—Silent.' You had to choose. Even then I thought it was unreasonable . . . Someone has a headache, someone has an appointment . . .

HERZEN Oh, shut up about your clock! (*to Ogarev*) Well . . . print it, then!

BAKUNIN (*joyfully*) You won't regret it!

HERZEN (*exasperated, affectionate*) Oh Michael! I shouldn't be impatient with you. You incubate the germ of a colossal activity for which there is no demand, but when I remember you in Paris . . . and your entire worldly goods were a trunk, a folding bed and a tin basin . . .

BAKUNIN Great days.

The Maid enters with glasses of tea.

TURGENEV (*to the Maid*)   'Tea! Thank you so much!' . . . You know, the Viardot's butler left them. He said they weren't gentlefolk, because Viardot spoke to him at dinner.

BAKUNIN   I'm afraid my establishment is complete. (*to Herzen*) What did you think of Korf? He's a real catch for us, an officer. I'm sending him to Wallachia, and then he'll look round in the Caucasus.

HERZEN   To Wallachia, and a look round in the Caucasus . . .

BAKUNIN   It's not amusing.

HERZEN   You've come across a shy young man who wants to prove his devotion by doing anything you tell him. He came to London to see the International Exhibition in Kensington, and you want him to go to Wallachia. What for? You know you don't want anything in Wallachia.

BAKUNIN   How do you know I don't?

HERZEN   Because if you did, you'd have been telling me about it incessantly for the last week. And all this nonsense with secret journeys, secret codes, false names, invisible ink—it's just children's games. No wonder Liza is the only one of us who has no doubts about you. You send people letters in code and put the code in the same envelope so the person can read the letter.

BAKUNIN   I admit that was a mistake, but what about you?— all you do is fill the *Bell* with futile discussions about peasants—who can't read it. I agree with Turgenev.

TURGENEV   Me?

BAKUNIN   It's all pedantry—of no practical utility.

HERZEN Thank you very much! I'm already being called a nihilist by (*to Turgenev*) your publisher. I'm to blame personally for the student demonstrations at home. St Petersburg is being burned down at my orders. And here I am—or rather, here is Ogarev—slaving over a petition to the Tsar to establish a council of all the classes to iron out the grievances . . . which Turgenev refuses to sign.

TURGENEV I do.

HERZEN Why? You believe in parliaments!

TURGENEV Yes, but you don't.

HERZEN I believe in this one as an expedient.

BAKUNIN But things are moving too quickly.

HERZEN Where? In Wallachia?

BAKUNIN Very well. My respect for you has no bounds. I sincerely love you. I hoped I could join your alliance, but your haughty condescension towards your . . . towards those who . . . well, look, it's best if we work independently and, if possible, remain friends. I'm sorry, but there it is. (*Bakunin leaves.*)

OGAREV Don't let him go like that.

HERZEN He'll be back tomorrow as if nothing has happened.

Ogarev, upset, hurries out after Bakunin.

TURGENEV (*to Ogarev*) Good night! (*Pause.*) I don't feel well.

Natalie, reacting like Ogarev, but with anger, leaves the room.

TURGENEV (*cont.*) Actually, I went to the International Exhibition at Kensington . . .

Natalie returns.

NATALIE Tata's waiting up for me. Will you let her go to Italy with Olga?

HERZEN So far, nobody's going to Italy.

NATALIE You can't stop Malwida from living where she wants.

HERZEN I can stop Olga from going with her. That woman asked if she could take Olga to Paris for the winter—now she proposes to take her to Italy to live, because *you*—

Natalie turns on her heel.

HERZEN (*cont.*) And now Tata wants to go with them.— Well, nobody's going, so she can't!

Natalie leaves.

TURGENEV At Kensington, every country in the world has a stand displaying its unique contribution to human ingenuity. But none of the exhibits on the Russian stand— the samovar, the bast shoe, the yoke bridle and so on—are actually Russian inventions. They all arrived centuries ago from somewhere else. It occurred to me, looking round, that if Russia had never existed, nothing in that great hall would alter by so much as a hobnail. God help us, even the Sandwich Islands are showing off some special kind of canoe. But not us. Our only hope has always been Western civilisation transmitted by an educated minority.

HERZEN What you mean by civilisation is your way of life, your comforts, your opera, your English gun, your books lying about on good furniture . . . as if life as evolved in the European upper classes is the only life in tune with human development.

TURGENEV Well, it is if you're one of them. It's not my fault. If I were a Sandwich Islander I expect I'd speak up for navigating by the stars and eighteen things you can do with a coconut, but I'm not a Sandwich Islander. To value what is relative to your circumstances, and let others value what's relative to theirs—you agree with me. That's why despite everything we're on the same side.

HERZEN But I fought my way here with loss of blood, because it matters to me and you're in my ditch, reposing with your hat over your face, because nothing matters to you very much—which is why despite everything we'll never be on the same side. Not everything in your precious civilisation is on display in Kensington . . . a whole exhibition's worth of shame-faced accommodations is missing. Praise the Lord but put your faith in Mammon. Think what you like but lie like everyone else. In politics, constant protest with constant obedience. Good taste is the artistic principle, and the supreme virtue is punctuality.

Tata runs barefoot, in a nightdress, to Herzen.

TATA Why can't I?—I'm nearly eighteen!—I'm going to be an artist, my whole life is at stake!

HERZEN Yes—yes—go! Olga, too! Paris or Florence, what's the difference? Tata, Tata, don't forget your Russian . . . (*He hugs her.*)

TURGENEV (*leaving*) When you were stuck in Russia . . . well, never mind . . . wake me for breakfast, if I'm not dead.

He goes out, passing Natalie, saying good night to her.

HERZEN (*weeps*) Oh, Natalie . . . !

Natalie comes forward but hesitates.

HERZEN (*cont.*)   Natalie! It's your Tata grown up!

Tata kisses Herzen and runs out, stopping to hug Natalie. Natalie comes forward. Something has tipped in her.

NATALIE (*jeers*)   'Oh, Natalie! It's your Tata grown up!'

Herzen is frightened.

HERZEN   How dare . . . how dare you . . .

NATALIE (*laughs, speaking offhandedly*)   Oh, Natalie was all right, she was just silly for a poke, and Herwegh was kingdom come.

HERZEN   Not another word.

NATALIE   She worshipped you. But it's no good worshipping her if you wait till she's dead. Good old George was an education on his knees, which of course is not in your character—

Herzen puts his hands over his ears.

NATALIE (*cont.*)   I didn't lose you Olga! Don't blame me! It was already too late! (*Natalie leaves.*)

AUGUST 1862

Herzen remains, with his hands over his face.

HERZEN   No! . . . No!

Ogarev is with him. He has an opened letter.

OGAREV   It's a disaster. The police were waiting for Vetoshnikov at the frontier. They knew. They must have had an agent placed among your visitors. The Third Section knows how to do these things, after all. They searched the flats of everyone mentioned in the letters Vetoshnikov was carrying, and they found more names . . .

HERZEN It was me who dragged in Chernyshevsky!—in a postscript!

OGAREV Sleptsov got away, to Geneva. He says there were thirty-two arrests in all . . . Land and Liberty has ceased to exist.

HERZEN (*angrily*) I said to you—the *Bell* can't help them by coming out for them, it can only ruin itself. And it has.

OGAREV (*defiantly*) Yes, we lost the liberals! And the patriots, when we came out for the Polish uprising! So what? We're not publishers, we're supposed to be revolutionaries with a magazine, aren't we? Sasha, Sasha, don't you know? The boys who are under arrest, they're us when we climbed to the top of the Sparrow Hills and swore to avenge the Decembrists. (*Ogarev leaves.*)

SEPTEMBER 1864

Night. Natalie, in a nightdress, comes to Herzen.

NATALIE I can't sleep. (*playing a child*) I want, I want!

HERZEN (*gently*) Yes . . . yes . . . go back to bed. I won't be long.

NATALIE You really won't?

HERZEN I promise.

NATALIE Everything will be well again if we go to live in Switzerland. I know it will. I'll be different there. Why not? Why not?

HERZEN Yes! Why not? Nick doesn't want to leave, but he'll come if he can bring Mary. Ciernecki objects that the scenery won't compare with Caledonian Road, but he says he can move the press. Perhaps we can save the *Bell* by printing a French edition . . . and in Geneva there's hundreds of exiles from Russia now.

NATALIE You'll be nearer Tata and Sasha. We can all be happy again!—and what's there in England that you'll miss?

HERZEN (*thinks*) Colman's mustard.

One of the twins starts crying distantly in an upper room.

NATALIE It's Lola Girl. I'll settle her. The twins can have their third birthday in Paris on the way! Paris, Alexander!

Natalie leaves.

Ogarev enters.

HERZEN (*to himself*) Do you remember, Nick? (*Herzen follows Natalie.*)

OCTOBER 1864

Night.

Mary joins Ogarev, who has had too much to drink. He sings a snatch of Russian.

MARY What have you done with Henry? I sent him to the Lamb to fetch you.

OGAREV They won't serve me in the Lamb after my incident. They cannot distinguish between a medical condition and inebriation. For example, this is inebriation.

MARY   Is it? I'd called it soused. Oh, Nikholai Whatsitwhich!

OGAREV   Yes, I was once the owner of four thousand serfs. My redemption is slow but steady.

MARY   And now he wants me and Henry to go and live on an alp.

OGAREV   Not an alp, a lake, beautiful, they say. Let's sit down and discuss it. (*He lies on the ground.*) It's a sad Russian story. My wages come from the *Bell,* from Alexander's pocket. But . . . we can stay behind in London if you prefer.

MARY   And do what? I'm not going back to work!

OGAREV   The cows are noted for their beauty.

MARY   What do they speak there, Swiss?

OGAREV   They don't speak, they're cows, but in Geneva French is spoken.

MARY   I never did French.

OGAREV (*straight*)   I remember.

MARY (*cross*)   Any more of that and you can go on your own.

OGAREV   Mary, Mary . . . I won't go anywhere without you.

MARY   'Course not. You wouldn't last a week.

She hauls him up and helps him out.

MARY (*cont.*)   My Russian aristocrat.

OGAREV   We were only noble. I was a poet.

MARY   An aristocratic Russian poet . . . I wouldn't have dared make it my dream . . . and look, it's just life, life, after all.

APRIL 1866

A revolver shot . . . the attempted assassination of Tsar Alexander.

MAY 1866

Geneva. A café-bar.

Sleptsov, last seen four years earlier at Herzen's house, is waiting at a table . . . with a copy of the Bell. *He turns the pages listlessly. Herzen arrives.*

HERZEN   I'm afraid I've kept you, Sleptsov.

SLEPTSOV (*shrugs*)   But you're here.

HERZEN   You're reading the *Bell?*

SLEPTSOV   It was left in the rack. I expect you left it. Nobody is reading the *Bell*.

HERZEN (*pause*)   You said it was urgent.

SLEPTSOV   I'd like a *vin rouge*.

HERZEN   They probably have that, you could ask.

SLEPTSOV (*laughs*)   I'm sorry my nihilist manners aren't up to the company of a millionaire revolutionary.

HERZEN   What is it you want?

SLEPTSOV   Your fraternal support. Four hundred francs.

HERZEN   For what?

SLEPTSOV   To send to our comrades at home, and to publish a thousand copies of our pamphlet about Karakozov's assassination attempt on the Tsar.

HERZEN If your pamphlet says Karakozov was a deranged fanatic, and his revolver shot a useless stupidity which won't advance the fall of the Romanovs by a single day—that it was, in fact, an attempted murder, which (*pointing to the sky*) hit the crow instead—yes, I'll give you four hundred francs.

SLEPTSOV (*calmly*) No, it doesn't say that.

HERZEN Read my article. At least my shots at the Tsar hit their target.

Sleptsov laughs.

HERZEN (*cont.*) Your hero Chernyshevsky would agree with me. He was against terrorism. He and I agreed about things much more than we disagreed. We were a mutual complement to each other.

SLEPTSOV It's difficult to ask him, since he's doing fourteen years' hard labour. Isn't it? But you and Chernyshevsky? Allow me to tell you what I think about that. Between you and Chernyshevsky there is nothing in common. In your philosophy of life, your politics, your character, in the smallest details of your private life, you and Chernyshevsky are as far apart as it's possible to be. The young generation has understood you, and we have turned away in disgust. We don't care about your tedious, hackneyed, sentimental addiction to reminiscence and to ideas which are extinct. We have left you far behind, and you refuse to notice. You flap your wings and dream that you are still our leader and guide. Come down to earth. You're a poet, a storyteller, an orator, anything you please, but you're not a political leader or thinker, let alone the high priest of Russian socialism. Our future is not tied to the slow movements of blind, dumb, subterranean forces. We're taking it in hand. Don't you understand? To us,

Tsar Alexander and Herzen are the dance that's outlived its time. So, forget that you're a great man. What you are is a dead man. (*Sleptsov leaves.*)

AUGUST 1868

Switzerland.

Herzen, aged fifty-six, and less than two years from death, sits in the garden of a rented château near Geneva. Liza, aged nearly ten, comes backwards into view, dragging on a long halter. Sasha, now twenty-nine, enters accompanying his pretty Italian wife, TERESINA, who is pushing a baby carriage.

LIZA   Oh, come on!

SASHA   What are you doing with her?

LIZA   I'm going to milk her.

SASHA   She hasn't got any milk.

LIZA   How do you know?

SASHA   She hasn't had any babies.

LIZA (*amazed, enlightened*)   What? Oh . . . Is that why Teresina has milk . . . ? (*The halter is jerked out of her hand, and she chases it out of sight.*)

TERESINA   *Che cosa ha detto di me?* [What did she say about me?]

SASHA (*fondly*)   *Niente* . . . [Nothing.]

TERESINA   *Ha detto il mio nome.* [She said my name.]

SASHA   *Vuole mungere il vitello e non ha capito per il latte materno.* [She wants to milk the calf, and she didn't understand about mother's milk.]

They laugh quietly together, Teresina shyly. Louder is the sound of Natalie rebuking Liza. Natalie enters in nervous tearful distress.

NATALIE Why can't she have a dog?

SASHA (*to Natalie*) Calm down, it's all right.

NATALIE Is it? It is, isn't it? (*She looks into the pram.*) I murdered my two little ones, you know.

SASHA Now, stop.

NATALIE (*to Teresina*) I killed them with wanting my own way.

SASHA Teresina doesn't know French, she only speaks Italian.

NATALIE Huh! She doesn't even speak Italian. (*loudly for Herzen*) You disappointed your father. An Italian peasant for the wife of a Herzen!

HERZEN I . . . That's enough!

Natalie starts weeping again.

NATALIE I'm sorry, I'm sorry.

SASHA She's not a peasant. She's a proletarian.

Sasha and Teresina continue out of view.

NATALIE (*to Herzen*) You said wait until spring, and I said no, no, I want to leave now, straightaway, I want, I want . . . You said travel straight through to the south, and I said no, no, I want to see Paris again, I want, I want . . . and in Paris diphtheria was raging, and it took away our Lola Boy and Lola Girl . . . Why did you let me have my way?!

HERZEN Natalie . . . what's the use . . . ? Natalie . . .

NATALIE I am not the real Natalie. The real one is in the sky. (*Natalie meanders away into the further garden.*)

HERZEN (*calls*) Tata . . . Tata . . . !

Tata comes. She is twenty-three, and now Herzen's helpmate and confidante.

TATA I'm here . . . what is it?

HERZEN Has Olga come?

TATA No, not yet. Ciernecki came with something for Nick—he brought Bakunin, too.

HERZEN Bakunin? It's a family gathering, a holiday—

TATA He's going back with Ciernecki in a little while—it'll be good for you to have Bakunin to argue with. We're boring for you, and you're being so good . . . (*She kisses him.*)

HERZEN You'll bring Olga straight out when she comes? Perhaps the carriage wasn't at the station . . .

TATA I'm sure it was. I'll go and keep a lookout.

Tata leaves. Ogarev and Bakunin enter. Ogarev is sockless and has a stick, which he gives to Bakunin while he opens a crumpled parcel.

OGAREV (*pleased*) Mary's found my socks. I thought I'd seen the last of them. I had them on before I fainted. Did she get them from the police station, I wonder?

BAKUNIN Natalie is openly living with Herzen, so why can't you bring Mary? There's no logic to his sense of propriety.

OGAREV Well, don't make a fuss . . . (*approaching Herzen*) Look who's here.

HERZEN Oh . . . it's the International Brotherhood of Socialist Democrats, and he's got Ogarev with him.

BAKUNIN I've dissolved the Brotherhood. My new organisation is the Social–Democratic Alliance. Would you like to join?

Ogarev and Bakunin take chairs. Ogarev, with a little difficulty, puts on the socks.

HERZEN What are your aims, precisely?

BAKUNIN Abolition of the state by the liberated workers.

HERZEN That's reasonable.

BAKUNIN Now you have to give me twenty francs.

HERZEN I'll give you a copy of the *Bell*. It's the last one. They don't want us in Geneva, neither in Russian nor in French. I don't know why I came here. The Russians treated me with contempt so long as my purse was open to them. I gave and gave until I was tired of giving. And then they really turned on me. These 'new men' are the syphilis of our revolutionary lust. They spit on everything beautiful or humane, past or present.

BAKUNIN The old morality has gone, the new one is still being formed. They're caught between. But they've got courage and passion. There's always a touch of senility in hatred of the young. My youngest recruit is only sixteen.

OGAREV You mean Henry?

BAKUNIN Every voice is going to count. I'm in the process of turning the Alliance into the Geneva Section of Marx's International Working Men's Association.

HERZEN   But . . . Marx wants to take over the state, not abolish it.

BAKUNIN   You've put your finger on it.

HERZEN   On what?

BAKUNIN   That would be telling.

HERZEN   But I'm a member.

BAKUNIN   Yes, but inside the Alliance is a Secret Alliance!

HERZEN   How much is the subscription?

BAKUNIN   Forty francs.

HERZEN   No, I don't think so.

BAKUNIN   Well, I'll tell you anyway.

HERZEN   Oh, really, this is too much!

BAKUNIN   Marx doesn't know it, but the Alliance is going to be the Trojan horse inside his citadel! I really have a lot of respect for Marx. We are both out to free the workingman. But Marx wants to free the workers as a class, not as individuals. His freedom is regimentation by a workers' dictatorship. But true freedom is spontaneity. To be answerable to authority is demeaning to man's spiritual essence. All discipline is vicious. Our first task will be to destroy authority. There is no second task.

HERZEN   But your—*our*—enemies in the International number tens of thousands.

BAKUNIN   This is where my Secret Alliance comes in—a dedicated group of revolutionaries under iron discipline, answerable to my absolute authority—

HERZEN Hold on . . .

BAKUNIN Marx's day is done. Everything's coming together but for a few tiresome necessities. This is the last thing I'll ever ask of you—

He is interrupted by Tata coming from the house, preceding Olga. There is a general influx . . . Malwida, Sasha and Teresina, Natalie, who is somewhat recovered, and Servants bringing a considerable tea to a garden table towards which everybody is drawn—Olga and Malwida in due course. Herzen is brought alive by Olga's arrival. He goes to meet her. They kiss.

HERZEN (*rapidly*) Ya nye ooslýshal ekipázh! Tibyá vstrecháli na stántsii? I fsyó byló fparyádkye na granítse? Kak ty kharashó i módno adyéta! Shto? Shto tabóy? [I never heard the carriage! Was the carriage at the station? Was everything all right at the frontier? You look like a lady of fashion!—What? What is it?]

Olga glances, embarrassed, at Malwida.

HERZEN (*cont.*) Oh . . . you've forgotten Russian?

OLGA It's only that . . . Malwida and I are fluent Italians now!

HERZEN Well, why not?—We talk French half the time! The main thing is you're here. (*to Malwida*) Welcome!

SASHA (*to Olga*) You're an auntie!

Olga responds appropriately to Teresina and the pram. She already knows Teresina.

MALWIDA My, such opulence, Alexander! We're not used to it. How long have you taken the château?

HERZEN Just for the month. Your room has a view of the lake.

SALVAGE

MALWIDA We don't mind sharing.

Malwida joins the group. Herzen resumes his chair, somewhat apart from the tea table where the eight others—Liza absent—get into conversation . . .

SASHA (*to Bakunin*) Twenty francs? I'm not really interested in politics—I lecture in physiology.

NATALIE (*to Ogarev*) Tata did a lovely painting of her—that's how Sasha met her.

OGAREV Are you still painting and drawing?

TATA No. I wasn't good enough.

NATALIE Nonsense. (*to Herzen*) Come on, Alexander . . .

BAKUNIN Seven degrees of human happiness! First, to die fighting for liberty; second, love and friendship; third, art and science; fourth, a cigarette; fifth, drinking; sixth, eating; and seventh, sleeping.

Applause and dissent.

OGAREV First, love and friendship . . .

MALWIDA First, to raise a human being to the highest degree of which she is capable!

NATALIE Alexander . . .

TATA Let him he. He didn't have a good night.

NATALIE Well, who did? Where's Liza? My head aches.

MALWIDA (*to Natalie*) I'm a firm believer in flannel.

Herzen is asleep. Turgenev and Marx, who have strolled into view like mismatched friends, are Herzen's dream.

HERZEN Marx!

They ignore him.

TURGENEV Dobrolyubov once referred to me in the
Contemporary as . . . well, he was dead at twenty-six,
consumption, poor fellow, so who am I to complain? . . .
but he called me 'A fashionable novelist trailing in the wake
of a female singer and arranging ovations for her in
provincial theatres abroad . . .' I thought I might go and live
in the Sandwich Islands. What do you think?

MARX The Sandwich Islands? Like Russia, and for the same
reason, the Sandwich Islands are irrelevant. Considered as a
social class acting out its destiny in a struggle with the class
above, the proletariat of the Sandwich Islands is not as yet
significant. I couldn't recommend it, you'd miss all the fun.
None of us may live long enough, but when it comes, the
cataclysm will be glorious . . . Every stage leads to a higher
stage in the permanent conflict which is the march of
history. Industrialisation, ever expanding to feed the markets
for canoes, cooking pots, samovars . . . and ever contracting
to drive out competition . . . alienates the worker more and
more from the product of his toil, until Capital and Labour
stand revealed in fatal contradiction. Then will come the
final titanic struggle, the last turn of the great wheel of
progress beneath which generations of toiling masses
perished for the ultimate victory. Now at last the unity and
rationality of history's purpose will be clear to everyone—
even—finally—to the last Islander and to the last *muzhik*.
Everything that seemed vicious, mean and ugly, the broken
lives and ignoble deaths of millions, will be understood as
part of a higher reality, a superior morality, against which
resistance is irrational—a cosmos where every atom has
been striving for the goal of human self-realisation and the

culmination of history. I see the Neva lit by flames and
running red, the coconut palms hung with corpses all along
the shining strand from Kronstadt to the Nevsky Prospekt
. . .

HERZEN (*to Marx*)   But history has no culmination! There is
always as much in front as behind. There is no libretto.
History knocks at a thousand gates at every moment, and
the gatekeeper is chance. We shout into the mist for this
one or that one to be opened for us, but through every gate
there are a thousand more. We need wit and courage to
make our way while our way is making us. But that is our
dignity as human beings, and we rob ourselves if we pardon
us by the absolution of historical necessity. What kind of
beast is it, this Ginger Cat with its insatiable appetite for
human sacrifice? This Moloch who promises that
everything will be beautiful after we're dead? A distant end
is not an end but a trap. The end we work for must be
closer, the labourer's wage, the pleasure in the work done,
the summer lightning of personal happiness . . .

Marx and Turgenev ignore him and stroll away.

Herzen half falls out of his chair. Ogarev sees him and comes to him.

HERZEN (*cont.*)   (*awake*) Nothing, nothing . . . The idea will
not perish. The young people will come of age.

OGAREV   Whose fault is it we didn't carry them with us? We
knew what we were aiming for, but how were we supposed
to get it?—by revolution?—by Imperial decree?—a
constitution? What do you believe? I ask you seriously
because I no longer understand.

HERZEN   We have to open men's eyes and not tear them out
. . . and if we see differently, it's all right, we don't have to
kill the myopic in our myopia . . . We have to bring what's

good along with us. People won't forgive us. I imagine myself the future custodian of a broken statue, a blank wall, a desecrated grave, telling everyone who passes by, 'Yes—yes, all this was destroyed by the revolution.'

BAKUNIN (*lighting a cigarette*)   At last, the happy moment

NATALIE   There's going to be a storm.

Liza enters with a broken halter.

LIZA (*showing the broken rope*)   *Smatrí, slamálsa!* [It broke!]

HERZEN   *Ty nye patselóoyesh minyá?* [Will you give me a kiss?]

LIZA   *Da!* [Yes!]

She kisses him like a tomboy.

Summer lightning . . . and cheerful responses of fright . . . then thunder and further responses . . . and a quick fade.

The End.